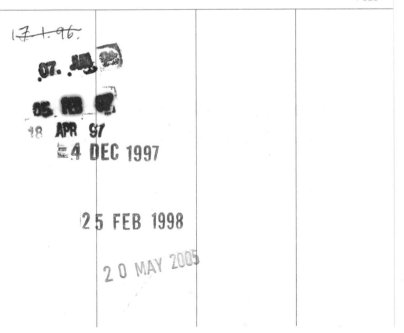
ISBN 0 901454 59 1

Contents

Tables and Figures

1 Executive Summary

1.1 Introduction

This is the report of a study of the housing needs of people with a visual impairment. The study was carried out by the Royal National Institute for the Blind (RNIB) and commissioned by the Housing Corporation.

1.2 Blind and Partially Sighted People in Great Britain

(i) Official information sources on blind and partially sighted people in Great Britain are of poor quality. The RNIB Needs Survey is the only contemporary and comprehensive source of information concerning the incidence of visual impairment, the lifestyles of blind and partially sighted people and their attitudes.

(ii) There are approximately 1 million people in Great Britain with a visual impairment, rendering them eligible to be registered as blind or partially sighted. Local authority maintained registers have approximately 250,000 people on them.

(iii) Approximately 750,000 households in Great Britain contain a person who is registerable as blind or partially sighted.

(iv) Blind and partially sighted people are disadvantaged in many ways as a consequence of their visual impairment, experience problems relating to mobility, isolation, low incomes and deprivation, and frequently inadequate access to housing.

1.3 Housing Needs of Visually Impaired People

(i) Appropriate housing is a basic human need. Visually impaired people require fair access to the general housing market and measures which reflect the housing-related consequences of visual impairment.

(ii) Enabling access to housing opportunities is, in essence, an equal opportunities matter.

(iii) Visual impairment can give rise to specific housing-related needs. These may include the need for appropriate design and adaptation of housing and the provision of housing, accompanied by appropriate management and care support.

(iv) Many visually impaired people prefer to live integrated into the community, not in a segregated setting.

(v) Information in appropriate and accessible formats is crucial in enabling access to appropriate housing.

(vi) Affirmative action is needed on the part of housing providers to ensure that blind and partially sighted people gain fair access to appropriate housing.

1.4 Identifying and Meeting Housing Need

(i) A range of agencies is responsible for provision of non-owner occupied housing in Great Britain. These include local authorities, housing associations and the Housing Corporation. Collaboration between agencies at all levels is of fundamental importance in identifying the housing needs of visually impaired people.

(ii) Local authorities play a pivotal role in collecting information on local housing need and in defining housing need at this level.

(iii) Housing associations play a crucial role in providing social housing generally and to special needs groups in the community.

(iv) Systems employed for identifying and subsequently meeting the housing needs of blind and partially sighted people are, on the evidence of this research, flawed by basic inadequacies in the systems of information collection and analysis. As a consequence, the housing needs of blind and partially sighted people are not accurately understood or met.

1.5 Awareness of Housing Need and Housing Provision

(i) Housing associations, as potentially key agencies in providing housing to visually impaired people, are heavily dependent upon local authorities for information and the setting of local housing needs priorities.

(ii) Housing associations tend to produce little information themselves which describes local housing needs generally. On the evidence from this research, hardly any information on the housing needs of blind and partially sighted people is produced.

(iii) Within generalist housing associations, the level of understanding of the housing needs of blind and partially sighted people tends to be limited. Few associations appear to take affirmative action relevant to blind and partially sighted people.

(iv) Blind and partially sighted people do not form a housing priority group within local authorities under current priority needs arrangements.

(v) Overall, the system for identifying and meeting the housing needs of blind and partially sighted people through housing provision is compromised by the absence of quality information, and is often fragmented. Blind and partially sighted people tend to fall through the net.

1.6 Housing Visually Impaired People: Access and Design

(i) Improving general access to housing for blind and partially sighted people will require revisions to the management information and assessment systems employed by local authorities and housing associations.

(ii) Affirmative action is required on the part of local authorities and housing associations. The provision of information on housing opportunities and options in appropriate and accessible formats is of paramount importance.

(iii) Improving blind and partially sighted peoples' access to the general housing market is a major priority. Also a priority is improving the extent to which design features which reflect the consequences of visual impairment are incorporated into the design of new housing and the adaptation of existing stock. Specific design aspects relate to lighting, signage, textural and tactile coding and design of space and layout.

1.7 Recommendations

(i) Recommendations are made at the conclusion of this report, which stem directly from the findings of the research.

(ii) Recommendations are made concerning:-

(a) The role and work of the Housing Corporation.

■ The Housing Corporation's Performance Standards should be amended to specifically refer to visually impaired people and their housing needs.

■ The Housing Corporation's Performance Review procedures should be amended to reflect the incidence and housing needs of visually impaired people.

■ The Housing Corporation should amend its Scheme Development Standards to incorporate good practice guidelines, designed to produce better practice amongst housing associations concerning blind and partially sighted people.

■ Future reviews of the Performance Audit visit manual should include the development of indicators relevant to blind and partially sighted people.

■ The Corporation should consider ways of making available resources for the development of new housing opportunities for blind and partially sighted people, where it can be demonstrated that specific development and provision is appropriate.

(b) The role and work of local authorities.

■ Local authorities should take steps under the community care planning programme to rapidly improve registration procedures.

■ Local authorities should adopt a policy for providing information on housing and housing opportunity in appropriate media.

■ Training in the housing needs of blind and partially sighted people should be a high priority.

■ Local authority housing departments should develop good practice guidelines relating to sensory impairment.

(c) The role and work of housing associations.

■ The registering and analysis of enquiries is an area which could be improved.

■ Housing associations should provide housing information in an appropriate medium and ensure that visually impaired and disabled people are reached by promotional material.

- Housing associations should develop an equal opportunities policy with regard to people with a visual impairment.

- Access to housing association offices should be enabled through appropriate design.

- Housing allocation policies should be vetted to ensure that they do not discriminate against people who have a visual impairment.

- 'No pets' rules should be waived with regard to people with a visual impairment who need a guide dog for mobility purposes.

- Design guidelines and briefs should include all of the issues that are relevant to people with a visual impairment.

- Training in visual disability awareness should be supplied to all appropriate housing staff.

- Repairs and maintenance issues should be dealt with in such a way as not to disadvantage people with a visual impairment.

- Allocation procedures should be monitored on an on-going basis to ensure that blind and partially sighted people receive fair access to housing.

- Associations should incorporate design features relevant to blind and partially sighted people in all new build schemes.

2 Introduction

2.1 Research Brief

This is a report of a study of the incidence of visually impaired people in Great Britain, their housing needs and the policies and procedures currently employed to identify and meet these needs. Specifically, the brief for the study included:

- Establish the numbers of blind and partially sighted people in England by Housing Corporation region and, if possible, by local authority administrative unit.

- Estimate the numbers of households containing a blind or partially sighted person currently housed by registered housing associations in England.

- Identify and describe key aspects of visually impaired people's lifestyles and housing needs.

- Describe and review practice in the allocation and management of housing for people with a visual impairment.

- Establish whether improvements to Housing Corporation guidance to housing associations on design issues is required.

2.2 Methods and Sources

Primary sources of information in this study were:

- All published data sources on the incidence of visual impairment.

- Literature relating to levels of housing need experienced by blind and partially sighted people.

- Semi-structured interviews with the Housing Corporation's regional offices and officers and a sample of housing provision agencies, including housing associations and local authority housing departments.

- Semi-structured interviews with blind and partially sighted people and housing association tenants.

2.3 Interview Samples

Interviews were held with Housing Corporation officials at national and regional levels. Participating respondents are as listed at Appendix 2(i).

Additionally, officers of the National Federation of Housing Associations and Chartered Institute of Housing were interviewed. Participating respondents are as identified at Appendix 2(ii).

A cross-sectional sample of housing associations was developed to form the base for data collection concerning housing association policy and provision. The sample was not intended to be statistically random, but was designed to include:

- Both specialist and generalist providers.

- Include large (national) and small (localised) providers.

- Include both urban and rural providers.

- Provide a national geographical spread.

The sample was approved by Housing Corporation officials; details of participating respondents are found at Appendix 2(iii).

A semi-structured interview schedule was developed and approved by Housing Corporation officials. This provided the core interview resource for researchers in the field and, in practice, worked very satisfactorily. All interviews were recorded on tape, transcribed and subsequently analysed to produce information relevant to the study. No statistical analysis was performed using the material derived from the interviews. The interview schedule is found at Appendix 2(v).

Discussions were held with local authority housing and social services officials concerning matters of allocation, management and design and, specifically, information collection and dissemination. Also covered were communication and co-operation arrangements with housing associations.

Interviews and group discussion sessions were held with blind and partially sighted people and housing association tenants, the aim being to gather data on their experiences of the housing provision system, their perceptions of this system, and design aspects relating to housing. Interviews and group discussion work was carried out at the RNIB's Garrow House Hostel in North Kensington and at the Gift of Thomas Pocklington in Holland Park. A total of 32 individuals contributed to this element of the work.

2.4 Non-Statistical Sources

There is a limited body of non-statistical material concerning blind and partially sighted people, their housing needs and the work of organisations in identifying and meeting these needs. This was used to inform the study generally and in the design of primary data collection. Main sources are identified at Appendix 4.

2.5 Research Resources

The research was undertaken by the Royal National Institute for the Blind (RNIB). RNIB's Corporate Planning and Evaluation and RNIB's Housing Service Departments created a team to do the work. The research was commissioned by the Housing Corporation, following a competitive selection procedure.

Specifically, those involved were Steven Cooper, Head of Corporate Planning and Evaluation, Katharine Sharpe, RNIB Researcher, Evaluation Studies, Jon Barrick, Manager, RNIB Housing Services, David Bryden, Senior Housing Officer (until 5/93), Jeremy Porteus (from 6/93) and Neil Crowther, Acting Senior Housing Officer. Close liaison with Steve Ongeri, Research Manager, Housing Management and Research Division, Housing Corporation, was of great importance in progressing and completing the work.

3 Blind and Partially Sighted People in Great Britain

3.1 Identifying Information Sources

An initial priority of this study was the identification of statistical and non-statistical sources which would enable:

- Establishment of the number of blind and partially sighted people in England by Housing Corporation region and, if possible, by local authority area. Readers should note that the Housing Corporation mandate relates only to England.

- An estimation of the number of households containing a blind or partially sighted person.

- Description of key aspects of blind and partially sighted people's typical lifestyle, the obstacles to independent living they may be expected to face generally, and in gaining access to housing specifically. The study revealed that there are few quality sources of data concerning these matters.

3.2 Main Sources of Information

There are at present three principal sources of data relating to blind and partially sighted people in Great Britain:

- Official statistics are produced annually by the Department of Health[1]; these are obtained from registration procedures used by local authority social service departments.

- The second principal source is the survey carried out by the Royal National Institute for the Blind (RNIB) into blind and partially sighted people[2]. This work is generally referred to as 'The RNIB Needs Survey'.

  This survey, the field work for which was undertaken in 1987/88, was the first large-scale investigation designed to establish the total numbers of blind and partially sighted people in Great Britain and gather data on their lifestyles, aspirations and the problems and barriers to progress which they face.

  A key finding of this study was that statistics on the incidence of visual impairment arising from the Local Authority registration were (as was suspected) a substantial underestimation of the visually impaired population. Registration statistics, as published by the Department of Health, produced a total of 162,000 people

registered as blind and 105,500 people registered as partially sighted, giving a total of 267,000 in 1991. The RNIB Needs Survey revealed that the estimated number of people with a registerable visual impairment was, in fact, in excess of 948,000 in Great Britain (see Table 1). There are, in addition, currently some 700,000 people who are not regarded as blind or partially sighted, but who cannot recognise a friend across a road[3]. This produces a total of about 1.7 million visually impaired people.

- The third principal source of information concerning blind and partially sighted people is the recently published data from the 1991 Census[4]. These most recent data, following secondary analysis using the RNIB Needs Survey incidence calculations, reveal that in 1991 a total of 868,200 blind and partially sighted people were living either in the community or in residential homes and institutions in England (see Table 1).

  Forecast calculations have now been completed based on the 1991 General Census, which reveal an overall increase in the visually impaired population of the United Kingdom between 1993 and the year 2000 of some 7.6% (see Table 2).

  Detailed calculations have been completed, providing an analysis of the incidence of blind and partially sighted people by local authority administrative unit and Housing Corporation Region. These statistics are found at Appendices 3(i) – 3(x).

3.3 Supplementary Sources of Information

Partial information on the incidence of visual impairment, lifestyles and services to blind and partially sighted people is available from several further sources. These include data made available by some District Health Authorities (DHAs) and Family Health Service Authorities (FHSAs). A number of voluntary organisations maintain some information (often local in its nature) on the numbers of blind and partially sighted people. Additionally, some local authority housing, education and social services departments collect statistics as do a very small number of specialist housing associations. The most convenient source for statistics from these agencies is the Chartered Institute of Public Finance Accountancy (CIPFA). Prior to the RNIB

Needs Survey, only two substantive reviews of information sources and their quality had been undertaken[5][6].

3.4 Problems with Data Sources

A number of problems affecting sources of information on blind and partially sighted people have been identified:

- Official (government and agencies) sources are based primarily on local authority registration procedures and returns made from these. Data from these sources are now acknowledged to substantially under-represent actual levels of incidence, and provide little information of a detailed nature.

- Collection of data by other agencies tends to be inconsistent in terms of the definition of visual impairment, data collection methodology, data collection frequency and aspects of lifestyle in relation to service need.

- Collection of incidence and lifestyle data lacks co-ordination in a national sense. No one agency thus far has been given responsibility for collation of statistics nationally.

  With reference to the housing needs of blind and partially sighted people, this (and previous) research has revealed that very little information is or has been produced by housing provision agencies or authorities. The actual incidence of visual impairment, lifestyles of blind and partially sighted people, and, specifically, their housing needs and experiences, continue to be an under-researched and thus unclear area. Recommendations in this regard appear in Section 9 of this report.

3.5 Blind and Partially Sighted People in Great Britain: The Overall Numbers

Table 1, abstracted from the RNIB Needs Survey, shows that in 1991/92 a total of up to 200,000 blind and partially sighted people lived in residential establishments. In addition, a further 777,000 lived in households in the community. We are, therefore, able to estimate that this figure (777,000) represents the number of households in Great Britain containing a person who was, or was eligible to be, registered as blind or partially sighted.

Table 2 contains data on the blind and partially sighted population in the United Kingdom by age with forecasts to the year 2000.

Further statistics on the blind and partially sighted population can be found in the Appendices to this report.

Table 4 contains data on the blind and partially population of England by Housing Corporation region. This table contains extensive data and, for this reason, is found at Appendix 3(I).

Table 1   The blind and partially sighted community—Great Britain 1991/92*

	Age 0-16	Age 16-64	Age 65-75	Age 75+	Total
Blind and partially sighted people living in the community	10-20,000	77,000	180,000	500,000	757,000-777,000
Blind and partially sighted people living in residential homes and institutions					150,000-200,000
Total					977,000
People with additional disabilities					
Blind and partially sighted plus hearing impairment		17,000	61,000	185,000	263,000
Total	16,000	48,000	122,000	340,000	526,000

Technical notes:
(i)   *The blind and partially sighted population of Great Britain comprises approximately 1.8% of the total population.
(ii)   Evidence of geographic variance: there is currently no empirical evidence to suggest any geographic variance in incidence of visual impairment. Prevalence rates are age-related (see Figure 1), areas with a higher proportion of elderly people will as a consequence have higher incidence of visual impairment.

Source:
Blind and Partially Sighted Adults in Great Britain: The RNIB Survey—Volume 1. Ian Bruce et al, HMSO 1991.

Table 2   Blind and partially sighted people in the UK—1993 – 2000

	1993	1996	1998	2000	Increase/ decrease %
Under 16	24,010	24,600	24,830	25,030	4.25
16 to 59	95,400	96,340	96,960	97,520	2.23
60-74	199,720	195,020	193,450	193,350	−3.30
75+	711,170	751,440	776,500	792,970	11.50
Total	1,030,300	1,067,400	1,091,740	1,108,870	7.63

Figures rounded to the nearest 10.
Sources:
RNIB Needs Survey Prevalence Index, OPCS 1991 General Census.

Table 5 contains detailed statistics on the blind and partially sighted population of England by Local Authority administrative unit. This table contains extensive data and, for this reason, is found at Appendices 3(II) – 3(X).

From these data, it will be seen that there are just under 1 million blind and partially sighted people in the United Kingdom at present. This is a figure which is forecast to grow to some 1.1 million by the year 2000.

3.6 Age and Gender Aspects

Within Great Britain's visually impaired population, older people are preponderant. There is a clear and acknowledged epidemiological association between old age and visual impairment. Older people are defined as those at or beyond retirement age, with very old defined as those who are 75 years plus. Although people aged over 75 make up only 8% of the general population, they comprise 66% of the visually impaired population. In contrast, people of working age (16-59/64) make up 74% of the

general population, but only 10% of the visually impaired population[7]. A relatively high proportion of visually impaired people report one or more additional physical disabilities or chronic conditions. The most commonly reported conditions being hearing impairment (22%) and mobility impairments, brought, for example, by arthritic conditions[8]. Figure 1 illustrates the age profile of the visually impaired population.

In each age group, research has shown that there are more visually impaired women than there are men. The differential is greater than that found in the general population and widens in the older age groups. Even in the 16 – 59 age group, where women make up half of the general population, within the visually impaired population, women make up 57%. Within the 75 plus age group, three out of four (75%) visually impaired people are women. This pattern is best explained by the longer general life expectancy of women over men and the epidemiological association between visual impairment and old age[9]. Figure 2 illustrates the pattern.

Figure 1

Age profile of the blind and partially sighted population (Private households in Great Britain)

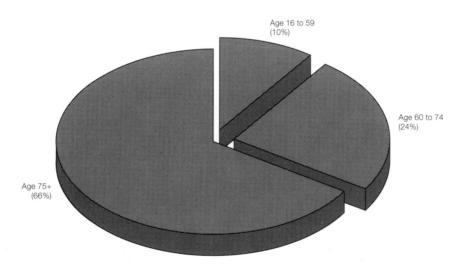

Age 16 to 59
(10%)

Age 60 to 74
(24%)

Age 75+
(66%)

Source:
Blind and partially sighted adults in Britain: The RNIB survey, volume 1.
I. Bruce, A. Mckennel, E. Walker. HMSO 1991

Figure 2

Distribution of the blind and partially sighted population by age and gender (Private households in Great Britain)

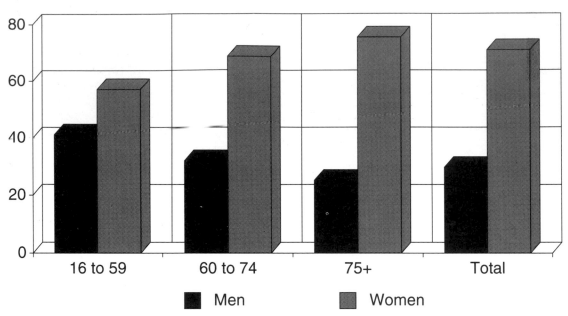

Source:
Blind and partially sighted adults in Britain: The RNIB survey, volume 1.
I. Bruce, A. Mckennel, E. Walker. HMSO 1991

3.7 Key Lifestyle Indicators

Visual impairment tends to bring major obstacles and disadvantages to those it affects:

- Isolation – The RNIB Needs Survey revealed that 250,000 older blind and partially sighted people in the community live alone[10].

- Isolation and mobility – about 400,000 older blind and partially sighted people experience not only isolation, but also significant mobility problems. During a typical week, nearly half of older blind and partially sighted people do not go outside their home or receive a visit from a friend, relative or neighbour[11].

- Mobility – virtually all blind and partially sighted people, particularly those who are older, report that they require assistance and/or aids with mobility[12].

- Independent living – 90% of blind and partially sighted people experience problems in day-to-day living, such as with personal care, domestic tasks, cleaning and communications[13].

- Information and awareness – research has shown that awareness of services and resources amongst blind and partially sighted people is extremely low. There is a strong correlation between registration and awareness of services. Typically, blind and partially sighted people are undemanding and have relatively low expectations[14].

- Income – only 25% of blind and partially sighted people of working age are in work at any given time. They tend to have an average weekly income of around 65% of the overall national average, a function of poor employment and equality policies. Older blind and partially sighted people experience greater hardship, with the majority living at or below the poverty line. Two-thirds of blind and partially sighted people over 65 live on a weekly income of less than £80. A substantial proportion of blind and partially sighted people of retirement age receive benefits in addition to their pension because of their low income. Nearly half receive some form of housing benefit and just over a quarter draw income support[15].

- Savings and reserves – blind and partially sighted people often have increased outgoings because of their disability, but rarely have the facility of savings or reserves to cushion their low income and pay for their extra needs. 63% of blind and partially sighted people of working age have savings of not more than £500. 80% of older blind and partially sighted people have savings of not more than £1,000(16).

3.8 Existing Housing Tenure Pattern and General Housing Need

A higher proportion of blind and partially sighted people are local authority tenants than is the case with the general population. Of blind and partially sighted people aged between 16-59, 40% live in local authority properties compared with 23% for the general population. The reduction of local authority housing stock and the unsuitability and expense of private rented accommodation means that blind and partially sighted people will become increasingly dependent on the only other viable source of accommodation, housing associations. Currently, however, only 5% of all blind and partially sighted people live in housing association accommodation. Within the working age group (16-59/64), this figure falls to only 1%.

To provide a context for this data, the General Household Survey indicates that 9% of all people live in housing association accommodation. The same survey indicates that 7% of working age people live in housing association stock.

Table 3 illustrates the overall pattern, including the fact that only 4% of blind and partially sighted people are owner occupiers with a mortgage; of these, the majority, as expected, are under the age of 60. Some 36% of the total blind and partially sighted population own their property outright; of this total, 70% are in the retirement age bands. However, a key point is that in these cases, research shows that property tends to have been inherited rather than purchased by the visually impaired owner[17]. Within the working age bands, 50% of blind and partially sighted people are owner occupiers, either with a mortgage or owning property outright. Here again, the inheritance point applies. The overall figure compares with one of 68% owner occupation for the general population.

Table 3 Tenure classification within three age groups of blind and partially sighted people in private households in Great Britain

	16-59 %	60-74 %	75+ %	Total %
Mortgagees	25	2	2	4
Outright owners	25	30	40	36
Local authority tenant	40	58	38	43
Private tenant	1	6	4	5
Housing association/charity tenant	1	0	5	4
Live with others	4	2	8	6
Other (e.g. tied)	4	2	3	3
Total	100	100	100	100
Base population	77,000	180,000	497,000	753,000

Source:
Blind and Partially Sighted Adults in Great Britain: The RNIB Survey—Volume 1, Ian Bruce et al, HMSO 1991. Columns may not add to 100 owing to rounding.

Blind and partially sighted people tend to have distinctive general housing needs. Gaining access to appropriately located, affordable and well equipped housing is an important need which affects all members of the community. Access to appropriate housing by blind and partially sighted people is affected by a wider range of factors. Research undertaken during the course of this study has enabled the development of a better understanding of these.

■ Access and the importance of information – interviews carried out during the course

of this study have confirmed that information, available in appropriate formats (for example large print, tactual or audio media), is a vitally important resource, but usually unavailable. Most people, when seeking accommodation either in the rented or owner occupied sector, rely on printed information, such as advertisements or brochures, as the first stepping stone. Blind and partially sighted people encounter problems with this, particularly when seeking to enter the private rented sector. The problem also affects the public rented sector: for example, where blind and partially sighted people apply to get into local authority or housing association accommodation, absence of documentation in accessible and appropriate formats often proves to be a major obstacle. In general, information in the right tactual and audio formats is not commonly available to blind and partially sighted people seeking access to housing.

■ Advice – awareness of access to sources of advice has long been known to be a problem. There are few sources of specialist advice and information available to blind and partially sighted people. The RNIB Housing Information and Advice Service is the only national provider. Generic sources of information such as Local Authorities and Citizen's Advice Bureaux are helpful, but are often unable or unequipped to provide information in appropriate formats. Networking, for example, for the purposes of referral between agencies, tends to be under-developed in relation to visually impaired people.

■ Location and access – blind and partially sighted people prefer, for reasons relating to convenience and mobility, to live in reasonably close proximity to key amenities, such as shops and leisure opportunities. Interviews and discussions have revealed that it can take a blind person up to two years to develop a 'mental map' of his/her residential environment. This can have a limiting effect on their housing opportunities.

■ Access and transport – given that, by definition, blind and partially sighted people do not drive vehicles and often have limited access to transport by car, public transport systems are of critical importance. Close proximity to good transport networks is crucial. Blind and partially sighted people, of preference, wish to be near effective transport, which in turn gives them access to amenities and employment opportunities. As with amenities, this factor can have a limiting effect on housing opportunities.

■ Employment – the closer that employment or employment opportunities are to housing for blind and partially sighted people the better. This is a view strongly expressed by blind and partially sighted people, linking into considerations concerning amenities and transport.

■ Environmental security – blind and partially sighted people have a heightened awareness of security and related issues, for obvious reasons. They prefer to live in areas which they are familiar with in terms of the layout of the environment, and comfortable in terms of incidence of crime and anti-social behaviour.

■ Design issues – a range of design issues relating to layout, adaptations and equipment and decor are covered in Section 7 of this report. Here, a number of specific internal environmental factors are summarised.

■ Security in the home – a key consideration, for example, intercoms are infinitely preferable to security spyholes.

■ Maintenance of property – clearly an issue for blind and partially sighted people, who often can neither detect the need for, or carry out, repair and maintenance work. There are repercussions here in the area of supportive management in housing association properties and also 'care and repair' schemes.

■ Noise insulation – given that in the absence of sight, hearing is often the key orientational faculty, adequate noise insulation is often important.

■ Hazard reduction – a range of design-related issues, such as colour and textural co-ordination, enabling safe movement around the home, are detailed in Section 9 of this report.

3.9 Key Points Summarised

(i) Information sources on the numbers of blind and partially sighted people in Great Britain have until very recently been scarce and lacking in detail.

(ii) There are, at present, approximately 1 million blind and partially sighted people in Great Britain.

(iii) Approximately 750,000 households contain a blind or partially sighted person, up to a further 200,000 blind and partially sighted community live in residential establishments.

(iv) Blind and partially sighted people experience a range of barriers and constraints in their participation in society generally.

(v)   Specific constraints apply to blind and
        partially sighted people in gaining access
        to housing opportunities.

(vi)   General support services and resources
        are often of major benefit in assisting blind
        and partially sighted people to lead a
        stable, productive life.

4 Defining and understanding housing needs of visually impaired people – key principles

4.1 Introduction

Appropriate housing is a basic human need. Visually impaired people require fair access to the general housing market and, in some circumstances, additional measures which reflect the specific housing-related consequences of visual impairment. These may reach beyond establishing access to the general housing market, and include housing design incorporating specific features.

4.2 Enabling Access to Housing

Access to housing for visually impaired people is, in essence, an equal opportunities matter. Agencies offering housing should demonstrate within their general policies and management practices a commitment to ensuring fair and equal access, and the avoidance of discrimination and causes of disadvantage. This is a key point in producing fair access to housing.

This applies to visually impaired people as to all others, and should be regarded as the base for housing provision to visually impaired people. Indeed, evidence from this research, other studies and other data suggests that a basic commitment to equal opportunities policy is often sufficient to ensure that visually impaired people gain fair access to the housing market and stock.

Data gathered from specialist visually impaired housing services reveal that up to 60% of visually impaired people of working age are confident enough to prefer a fully independent lifestyle and housing situation. They are secure enough to address the housing market as individuals without help from any further specific measures or assistance.

However, visually impaired people of working age comprise a minority of the total visually impaired population (see Table 3). Most visually impaired people are older, many live with other sensory and physical impairments.

This study, and others, has identified a number of major barriers frequently encountered by visually impaired people in gaining access to housing. Such barriers undermine the principle of equal opportunity in access to housing. These include: the environment (see Section 3), design aspects (see Section 7) and management aspects.

Specific problems have been identified relating to:

- Facilitating access through information in appropriate formats.

- The weakness or absence of proactive or affirmative 'marketing' strategies.

- Lack of continuity or networking between the range of organisations active in providing housing.

- Absence of accurate information on the incidence and needs of visually impaired people to provide a base for policy development and provision of appropriate housing.

- Lack of appropriate monitoring and quality control procedures designed to develop access to appropriately designed housing.

Each of these factors tends to work against the principle of equal opportunity in accessing housing. Each must be addressed in order to improve the situation.

4.3 Specific Needs and Facilitating Access to Housing

While an equal opportunity base for provision and access to housing is the primary objective, if specific needs can be defined by analysing the characteristics and lifestyles of a group within the community (beyond those required by people in general), it should be accepted that specific needs, in fact, exist.

This should not be seen as an alternative approach to an equal opportunities philosophy, but is, moreover, complementary to and conformal with it. Without an understanding of the diversity of groups of people, their varying needs and the positive actions required to provide for equality of opportunity and access, policies and practices will not be developed which work to enable the overall objective of equal opportunities.

The practical effects of visual impairment and the specific needs of visually impaired people are implied in the legislation through which health authorities and social service departments are encouraged or required to identify and meet these needs. Within health provision, ophthalmology departments and specialist hospitals exist to meet the fact and challenge of failing sight. There is significant investment in the prevention and care of blindness. Local authorities, as documented elsewhere in this report, have a statutory obligation to operate a register of blind and partially sighted people. Visual impairment precipitates problems in daily living, mobility and in communication, which vary from individual to individual in their effect and which are not impossible to deal with or compensate for with appropriate support. This support may be something as simple as prosthesis, for example a long white cane to aid mobility, or more complex electronic or computer based equipment to facilitate communication.

Affirmative action which facilitates access to housing may include:

- Information, raising awareness and access to housing – ensuring the information and material is available in appropriate formats within the context of proactive marketing and information strategies.

- Management – ensuring that housing providers manage their stock and relationships with visually impaired tenants in ways which reflect the needs of these tenants.

- Design – ensuring that the design of housing units reflect the range of physical consequences of visual impairment.

Action concerning all of these aspects can and should be taken in pursuit of the equal opportunities objective.

4.4 Role of Special Needs Scheme

The conventionally accepted notion of 'special care' in housing is linked to the view that individuals with 'special needs' have these needs most effectively met through specific supported schemes, such as housing with care, housing with 'extra care' or housing with management and support. Thus, for example, special needs housing schemes for people with significant physical impairment, such as wheelchair users have been developed, which provide good access to housing. Similarly, housing schemes for people with multiple disability, such as those operated by the Leonard Cheshire Foundation, provide access to appropriately designed and managed housing. Local Voluntary Societies for the Blind have built some schemes in the past, for example, facilities operated by the Pocklington Trust. Overall, however, the track record of both housing associations and local authorities in providing housing for blind and partially sighted people has, in fact, been very poor.

Summarised elsewhere in the report are the specific housing-related needs of visually impaired people, including assistance with independent living skills and equipment, communication issues, mobility skills and equipment. The solutions to the problem of meeting the special needs of visually impaired people are varied and diverse. Anecdotal evidence, including contact between blind and partially sighted people and RNIB's Housing Advocacy Service, indicates that only a proportion of visually impaired people believe that special housing schemes provide appropriate solutions for them. Many do not wish to reside in what they may regard as 'visually impaired ghettos'. However, organisations of visually impaired people and considerable numbers of older visually impaired people stress the case for specialist schemes, particularly for older people, where process of coming to terms with blindness in later life can be significantly aided by specialist assistance and environment. Visual impairment can and often does significantly compound the general consequences of old age and infirmity.

One group consulted during the course of the research, residents of housing operated by the Pocklington Trust[1], emphasised the relevance of special needs schemes for deaf, blind older people, a group largely ignored by housing providers. The particular communication needs of this group, along with their other difficulties, for example, frailty and mobility problems, meant that isolation in the community, often with inadequate support, was the worst housing option and yet the only one offered in practice. Housing schemes reflecting the specific needs of this group would have to be developed as regional or collaborative local authority sponsored ventures due to the small numbers of people involved.

This research confirms that older visually impaired people tend to have particular needs over and beyond those associated with old age. Existing supported schemes for older people usually do not, as a rule, make specific provision for the needs of their visually impaired residents. Examples of this were the failure to provide an appropriately designed environment, insufficient training for staff concerning visual impairment, inadequate care support services, and lack of appropriate communication systems. A significant number of older visually impaired people do believe that their specific needs would best be met within specially designed and managed schemes, offering appropriate design and care or support, whilst retaining an appropriate level of independence.

4.5 Meeting Specific Need Outside the Specialist Scheme Framework

Many visually impaired people exercise a will to live integrated in the community, in situations which would not be defined as 'special needs schemes'. This, however, does not necessarily mean that the need to support visually impaired people is no longer present. A number of local authorities, prompted by the Community Care legislation, are operating community care support teams addressed to those tenants and home owners whose visual impairment gives rise to the needs for support, but who wish to remain in their existing accommodation. Such initiatives are welcome and in themselves generate a need to further develop appropriate skills and knowledge within these teams with regard to visual impairment.

4.6 A Comprehensive Approach

Analysis of data from the RNIB Housing Advocacy and Helpline reveals that, of those seeking housing in non-specialist schemes, 40%(2) of callers sought independent housing, where support came as part of the tenancy package. This type of information indicates that the meeting of the special needs of visually impaired people requires a flexible approach based on an assessment of individual housing need and appropriate responses from housing management and community care agencies.

This report pinpoints inefficiencies throughout the 'system' of needs identification and housing provision for visually impaired people by housing associations and local authorities. Recommendations are made which address these inefficiencies.

These inefficiencies compromise the equal opportunities objective beyond a simple failure to recognise the specific consequences for individuals of being visually impaired. Specific needs exist, which unless addressed have the potential to undermine the visually impaired individual's ability to make use of the system of housing provision, however well it is designed in general. People with a visual impairment vary individually. Many have specific needs that require positive action to address these needs and overcome barriers which arise specifically because of their visual impairment.

An appropriate equal opportunities policy or approach is vital, but must be underpinned by a preparedness to identify specific needs, understand their practical consequences and take the appropriate action in devising housing arrangements. In this sense, there is no contradiction between equal opportunities as a fundamental approach and recognition of and response to specific needs.

4.7 Key Points Summarised

(i) Enabling access to housing by visually impaired people is a basic equal opportunities matter.

(ii) Many visually impaired people want to lead lives integrated into the community, not segregated.

(iii) Specific housing needs do arise from the consequences of visual impairment. This should be recognised as a fact.

(iv) Housing providers should take affirmative action to enable access to housing by visually impaired people, which reflect both an equal opportunities objective and specific needs as appropriate - a comprehensive service provision approach.

5 Identifying and Meeting Housing Needs: Current Arrangements

5.1 Introduction

Effective working relationships are the key to identification of housing needs, appropriate provision and good practice generally in social housing. Coherent and effective procedures are required to ensure that good working relationships between the Housing Corporation, local authorities and housing associations exist. Collaboration between these agencies relies heavily on access to robust information produced from effective and reliable sources. This is a prerequisite to policy development, housing provision and monitoring. This section of the report summarises the respective roles of housing organisations and the approaches (assessed as part of the study) to identify the housing needs of visually impaired people.

5.2 The Role of Local Authorities

Local authorities, and specifically local authority housing departments/services, are the main providers of social housing in Great Britain. Local assessment of housing needs and letting allocation is a primary responsibility of local authorities. A sound communication and working relationship between Housing Corporation regional offices and local authorities within their regions is of paramount importance in translating the Corporation's national strategy into investment and provision at the local level. For these purposes, information on local housing needs and provision is drawn primarily from local authority sources.

5.3 The Role of Housing Associations

Housing associations are important providers of housing in England. They work in conjunction with local authorities and with the Corporation to identify housing needs and develop investment and provision programmes designed to meet them. Many associations are essentially generic by character – that is providing low cost housing for individuals or families, on low incomes, for rent or sale. There are, in addition, a number of more 'specialist' or client specific associations that are seeking to work with groups within the community, such as people with physical impairments, the very old and frail and those needing specially designed accommodation.

5.4 The Role of The Housing Corporation

The Housing Corporation is the Government agency responsible for allocating and managing investment in social housing, specifically through registered housing associations. Its key tasks are currently:

- To co-ordinate allocation of resources within the Government's social housing programmes which are under its responsibility.

- To advise and support registered housing associations.

- To substantially strengthen the financial regulation of registered housing associations.

- To introduce and develop initiatives designed to further the interests of associations and their tenants.

- To collaborate with associations and other agencies to identify and subsequently work to meet special housing needs:

The Corporation has its headquarters in London, from which strategic management of the agency is exercised. Management of investment and operations is conducted through the Corporation's regional structure. At the time of field work, this comprised nine regional offices in England. A reduction to eight regional offices is planned for April 1995.

The Corporation interacts with local authorities and housing associations within its individual regions. Corporation regional policy is the result of national (governmental) policy priorities and targets and the local (regional) assessment and identification of social housing need. The Corporation's aim is the development of strategies and policies for housing investment and management which reflect policy from the national level, but which clearly emphasise regional and local needs. In addition, the Corporation has a wider policy generating role, the purpose of which is identification of major housing-related policy issues and the stimulation of debate and action in relation to them. This study represents an example of this work.

5.5 Monitoring

Monitoring of the activities of housing associations is a key activity of the Corporation. The main procedure now employed to this end is the Corporation's Performance Standards for Housing Associations and the Performance Standards Return (HAR14). This requires associations to supply detailed information on general management and financial aspects and in relation to key functional standards covering access to housing, management, property maintenance and development. Returns are collated centrally to produce an annual profile of associations in relation to performance standards. This system builds upon the earlier Performance Audit Manual (1992) and Performance Criteria for Housing Associations.

Monitoring of new lettings and relettings as distinct from existing tenancies is conducted using the Continuous Recording of Lettings System (CORE).

Both systems, however, do not at present capture data specifically on visually impaired people. Recommendations appear at Sections 9.2 and 9.6 in this connection.

5.6   The Housing Needs Index

Accurate information concerning local housing need, including household and demographic factors and housing stock characteristics, is crucial. So, also is a means of assessing priorities for stock regeneration investment. The Housing Needs Index (HNI) is the key mechanism developed and employed by the Corporation for this purpose, which is currently used to guide the application of investment at regional and local levels.

The HNI is a composite indicator of the nature and incidence of housing needs and problems in different geographical areas, and, as such, is used to guide the distribution to housing associations of the Corporation's programme of grants and loans for capital schemes. HNI does not currently include direct consideration of housing needs of visually or other sensorily impaired people. HNI came into existence in 1985 and has been used since that time. Minor modifications to its format were introduced in 1991. A further review of its make-up commenced in mid-1993 with a view to revising the indicator for use in the financial year 1996/7.

5.7   Influencing Local Housing Priorities

The schedule employed to guide interviews for this research included sections concerning the perceived role and use of the HNI. Some respondents (including Corporation respondents) indicated a perception of HNI as having a role(s) wider than guiding social housing investment. In one case, a respondent indicated that the HNI tends to generate discussion on wider housing needs, beyond investment priorities.

In another case, a respondent described how the presence of, for example, of a homelessness indicator in HNI influenced strategy definition at the local authority level, in the sense that bids for investment would then be made, which accentuated the incidence of homelessness in an area.

One respondent detailed a practice of systematic use of HNI at the individual local authority level to shape local housing priorities, with the aim of attracting investment.

The indicator was certainly not constructed by the Corporation with a view to pre-determining housing investment priorities in regions or local authorities. It is intended, rather, to be a reflection of needs identified at these levels. There was, nonetheless, some evidence that it is employed to construct local housing strategies in inappropriate fashions.

Concern was also expressed by several respondents about HNI's perceived failure to identify all housing needs, to be addressed by investment. Substantial hidden need is perceived, in no small measure, because robust information does not always exist to reveal such needs.

5.8   Assessing the Housing Needs of Visually Impaired People

Interviews conducted as a component of this research focused on the assessment of the housing needs of visually impaired people in practice. A number of themes were identified by very nearly all respondents:

- Local authorities – are seen as having a strategic enabling role in housing and are the primary source of information on housing needs in their area. Information tends to come to Corporation regions directly from local authority housing departments. Corporation regions also rely heavily on the local authority for general housing strategy for the region. Corporation regions unanimously perceive local authorities as the bodies ultimately responsible for gathering information on housing needs.

- Quality of information from local authorities – is perceived to be patchy and varies considerably, a situation which in itself creates significant problems. Local authorities gather information on the basis of their statutory functions and as a consequence of being subject to political pressures and lobbying. Some are thought to present information to Corporation regions, which may not always be a systematic and balanced illustration of housing needs. This is seen by some Corporation regions as an area requiring attention. Others adopt a reasonably pragmatic stance. A key point, however, is that poor information availability tends to mean that the identification of housing needs of visually impaired people is not always effective.

- Local surveys – some local authorities are known to undertake local 'needs surveys' on a systematic basis. These are perceived as useful and the basis for reliable and good quality information.

- Good practice models – Corporation regions suggest that local authorities should start producing clear and consistent approaches to needs assessment, which can be used as 'models' or examples of good practice. It is worth noting, however, that although the Corporation wishes to encourage a clear and consistent approach to needs assessment, none of the regions said directly what they require or mean by this.

- Liaison and consultation between the Corporation and local authorities. Corporation regions operate a structured programme of consultations with local authorities, based typically on quarterly meetings. The research interviews with Corporation respondents suggest that liaison between Corporation regions and local authorities in the form of housing departments, and particularly social service departments, is not always perceived to be totally effective. Outside of formal liaison arrangements, communications tend to be relatively informal. If anything, there is a perception that formal structures for liaison via local authority housing Departments concerning housing needs and information sources should be further developed.

- Further special needs research – none of the Corporation regions was, at the time of field work, involved in doing its own research into housing need. Regions can, however, recommend research subjects or areas within the Corporation; research into the housing needs of blind and partially sighted people was perceived by one Area Manager to be a high priority.

- Liaison with voluntary agencies – interviews provided evidence that this is often limited and inconsistent. The 'political' or campaigning nature of the activities of some community groups and organisations further affects this interface.

- Liaison and collaboration between the Corporation and housing associations – some specialist associations (for example Anchor Housing Association) provide information on their organisation's specialism to Corporation regions. The view to emerge in general from regions was that housing associations are informed about requirements in the district by the local authority, often without themselves having any primary input to defining these housing needs. Both Corporation and housing association interview respondents expressed reservations about the effectiveness of routine liaison, and specifically liaison concerning people with sensory impairments.

- Community Care – is widely perceived as the framework within which special needs information and assessment may see improvements. Overall, the picture to emerge is mixed, with information gathering and liaison arrangements concerning housing needs of visually impaired people varying considerably in nature and effectiveness.

5.9 Key Points Summarised

(i) Local authorities play a vital role in collecting information on local housing need.

(ii) Housing associations should, in theory, contribute to the development of local housing need priorities, but frequently channels of communication between them and local authorities do not facilitate this.

(iii) The Housing Corporation has an important role to play in supporting stock regeneration in the context of local needs priorities.

(iv) The quality of information on incidence of visual impairment and related housing needs is poor. This, combined with inter-agency collaboration, which may not always be effective, works to adversely affect the understanding of housing needs of visually impaired people, and provision for them.

6 Awareness of Housing Need and Housing Provision

6.1 Introduction

This part of the report deals primarily with policies and procedures at present employed, firstly by housing associations and secondly by local authorities, in providing housing for blind and partially sighted people. Material was gathered from the programme of interviews with housing association personnel and those working for local authorities and other sources. It should be noted that information was gathered during the course of structured interviews, which were not designed to produce data or other material in statistical forms, but to produce an overview.

6.2 Housing Associations and Use of Information Sources

All housing association respondents in the research sample perceived local authorities to be the major source of information and housing issues and needs. None regarded the Corporation as an important primary source of information.

A small minority of associations stated that they had, in the past, commissioned 'research', primarily amongst their own tenants, the focus usually being experience of the housing market generally. No evidence of recent research concerning the housing need of blind and partially sighted people was detected. One respondent association had commissioned research through a university, designed to identify 'dependent' groups in the association's catchment area.

Some evidence was found concerning influence on associations, by local voluntary groups, requesting information. In this way, attention may be drawn to housing needs of sensorily impaired people, but in an ad hoc manner.

Most respondent associations expressed reservations about their own basic administration and information systems. For example, some expressed the view that they could not quickly produce basic information on the numbers of tenants, numbers in households, or produce a comprehensive tenant profile. The research did not explore other administrative aspects, such as financial management or stock maintenance.

Uses of published external sources of information, for example official statistics, Chartered Institute of Public Finance and Accountancy (CIPFA) sources or research was explored. None of the respondent associations used these sources systematically or indeed occasionally. Few respondents had housing statistics and/or housing policy and management material in regular use within their agency. Research bodies, such as the London Research Centre and the Joseph Rowntree Foundation, were seen by some respondents as credible sources of information on housing needs.

All housing association respondents offered criticism concerning the quality of information on housing need provided by local authorities, some pointing to a paucity of relevant data. It seems clear that major improvements in the overall system of information gathering and distribution are required, rather than encourage a plethora of ad hoc arrangements and local studies.

6.3 Housing Associations and Awareness of Special Housing Needs in General

Most respondents interviewed were generalist housing providers. Awareness of special housing needs issues generally and special needs allocation policy was a specific line of enquiry in all interviews. This was probed as a precursor to enquiry concerning the housing needs of blind and partially sighted people. The overall picture to emerge was of relatively low awareness in both areas. Organisations working with some groups generally perceived to have 'special needs' produced documentation and material which may in fact overestimate the true nature of the situation – that is in terms of numbers in the special needs group and housing needs which exist. Similarly, evidence was collected which indicates that some groups under-state housing and other needs, perhaps because of weak organisation or lack of assertiveness. It may well be that weakness in the links between individuals, referral agencies and local authorities in part explain this situation. Awareness of Corporation special needs policy and the approaches adopted by local authorities in profiling special needs appeared to be particularly low and patchy. A number of respondents were unable to explain special needs policies and strategies defined, for example, by the Housing Corporation or local authority, to any extent at all, some were not aware such policies exist.

Of the total group of respondents, only four agencies were able to demonstrate what could be regarded as outline understanding of the role and application of the HNI. This in practice may not be that much of a problem in the sense that one might not automatically expect a housing association manager to understand the details of

HNI. Nevertheless, the level of awareness of special needs frameworks was not, on the evidence gathered from interviews, particularly high. This is particularly significant given that a considerable number of people with physical impairments also have visual impairment (see Table 1).

6.4 Housing Associations and Awareness of Blind and Partially Sighted People and their Housing Needs

A direct consequence of problems with information sources is that the majority of respondents, at the time of the field work, could provide no significant information on blind and partially sighted people at all in their area; only two respondent housing associations were able to say how many blind or partially sighted tenants they had at the time of interview.

One respondent agency, at the time of the field work, understood and described the connection between visual impairment and older age groups and made the link between this and the fact that a proportion of tenants in their mainstream accommodation were aged 75 plus.

Only one respondent agency currently provides information on its services in a format suitable for blind and partially sighted people (tape). Some respondents reported that previous attempts at consultation with visually impaired people and tenants had produced a 'negative' response to the offer of producing material in appropriate formats. They reported that people actually turned down their offer.

One respondent agency acknowledged the need to try and establish how many of its tenants may have sight problems as the base data required before deciding whether to produce information, such as tenancy agreements, in appropriate formats.

Most respondents pointed to local authorities as their only ready source of information on needs of blind and partially sighted people and made the point that, since little information emanates from this source, there is little they feel they can do. To this extent, a certain sense of resignation was detected.

One respondent agency was aware of the shortcomings of the Blind and Partially Sighted Register as the base mechanism for collection of statistics, and expressed the view that, in the local authority areas surrounding the agency, a large number of blind and partially sighted people who may need social housing do exist, that is more than the number in the register. This agency uses informal mechanisms for both identifying blind and partially sighted people and developing understandings of their needs; these mechanisms include social clubs, luncheon clubs and cultural activities.

In summary, therefore, awareness of the existence and housing needs of blind and partially sighted people was at a low level. Most respondent agencies had little or no basic information. Only one respondent agency, a specialist provider, could show information on, and an understanding of, the housing needs of blind and partially sighted people.

6.5 Housing Associations and Allocation of Housing

Most respondents demonstrated a clear understanding that allocation priorities in general are defined by local authorities and form the basis of their arrangements for referrals to associations.

All respondent associations develop letting and allocation policies through formal committee procedures. Procedures and allocation policy are in written form (as required by regulation).

Only one respondent association (a specialist agency for blind and partially sighted people) could demonstrate policies relating specifically to blind and partially sighted people. One respondent association operated a policy allowing for guide dogs when it usually operates a 'no pets' rule.

Allocation is typically based on referral from local authorities and other authorised referral agencies and is complemented by a range of assessment procedures. A key point, however, is that no evidence of specific, proactive, policies relating to blind and partially sighted people in allocation of housing was found amongst non-specialist providers. No evidence was found of procedures designed specifically to facilitate access to housing by blind and partially sighted people.

6.6 Housing Associations and Housing Design for Visually Impaired People

Awareness and understanding of design issues relating to the housing needs of blind and partially sighted people was found to be negligible. Only specialist agencies produced reference materials, such as design guides or design policy documents.

A limited amount of evidence of involving (via consultation) blind and partially sighted people in improving layout, design and management was found. Some respondents indicated that consultation occasionally takes place with community based groups which may help in revealing housing issues relating to visually impaired people. However, no systematic approach to developing knowledge in this connection was in evidence.

The most common response from respondents to questions in this area was that steps are taken to recognise the need for 'accessible homes' and the development of general good practice, rather than developing design measures aimed specifically at people with a sensory impairment or sight problem. The link between age and visual impairment was, as a rule, not clearly recognised by respondents, even those specialising in housing for the elderly.

6.7 Role of Local Authorities in Identifying and Meeting Housing Needs

Local Authorities have a key strategic and enabling role in housing provision:

- Housing departments are responsible for collecting and disseminating information on housing needs generally and on special needs.

- Social service departments are statutorily responsible for operating a Register of Blind and Partially Sighted People.

- Housing departments are statutorily responsible for managing current local authorities stock and, via identification of needs, development of new stock.

- Housing departments are responsible for developing a housing strategy for their area.

- This strategy should incorporate collaboration with voluntary agencies and housing associations.

- The strategy should also incorporate collaboration with the Housing Corporation and encompass capital development and housing improvement programmes (HIP) for special housing needs purposes.

- Local authorities exercise lettings nomination rights.

There are no statutory responsibilities relating to design issues concerning blind and partially sighted people which govern the work of the local authorities. The Health and Community Care Act 1992 requires local authorities to identify service needs or special needs groups, including blind and partially sighted people, incorporating special housing needs where, following assessments, it is determined that these exist.

Local authorities, therefore, hold the key information, strategy development and provision roles.

6.8 Assessment of Housing Needs of Visually Impaired People

Material gathered from the field work revealed this to be a highly problematic area. The Blind and Partially Sighted Register operated by local authorities is now acknowledged to be an inadequate measure of the incidence of visual impairment. The register is known to be a key process in triggering awareness of and access to further assessment and services, including housing. In many cases, however, people with a visual impairment are simply not registered with local authorities. Therefore, authorities do not know that there is a need, the scale or nature of the need, and where the need may be found.

Despite the fact that some local authorities have implemented district – wide housing needs assessments, this research indicates that it is not the norm for all local authorities to have proactive strategies for gathering information on the housing needs of visually impaired people. Many do not have robust data on basic numbers. A commonly detected approach appears to be to wait for the need to identify itself rather than to go out and find it. This finding conforms with data collected from housing associations on information concerning special housing needs and collaboration with local authorities, and also conforms with data collected from Corporation regional offices.

Special needs priorities complicate the situation in so far as they change frequently. In respondent authorities, top priorities for accommodation were homeless people and young single parent families. Elderly and multi-handicapped people featured at relatively low positions on current priority lists and blind and partially sighted people did not feature at all.

6.9 Waiting Lists, Housing Registers and Visual Impairment

Most local authorities operate a conventional points system based around property sizes, for example one, two or four bedroomed units, or older persons' accommodation. Typically, this incorporates a priority weighting according to 'housing need' and uses factors such as the size of the property, the condition of the property, the lack of washing and/or cooking facilities, overcrowding, and the length of the time on the register to determine an applicant's priority. Assessments are made for low, medium and high priority. Persons awarded a high priority are likely to be re-housed by an authority subject to the availability of suitable sized housing.

Visual impairment does not at present constitute a cause for classification under 'housing needs'. Consequently, local authorities are unable to identify a blind or partially sighted applicant unless an applicant supplies supporting documents, such as a letter from a doctor, social worker or eye specialist.

Some authorities issue medical priority forms which are completed by an applicant and her/his doctor and submitted with a waiting list application. The classification of visual impairment as a medical priority tends to vary from authority to authority. It does not automatically constitute a medical priority. Medical priority tends to focus on learning and physical disabilities and those people registered as disabled. Consequently, needs assessment for blind and partially sighted people appears to be inconsistent from area to area.

With many local authorities and housing associations moving towards integrated waiting lists, there is a need for improved indicators on housing registration forms to enable authorities to identify applicants' 'special needs' and to plan effective solutions in their area.

6.10   Housing Allocation

Typically local authorities use nominations to Housing Associations as well as directly controlling their own managed stock. In respondent associations, local authority nominations typically exceeded 80% of the total lettings in any given year. Allocation from approved referral agencies and direct applications is, therefore, marginalised by the number of referrals coming through from local authorities.

Respondents reported that this is a long-standing status quo. At the time of fieldwork, many local authorities gave high priority to accommodating homeless families and single people, creating a situation where this category tended to dominate the pattern of referrals to associations.

No respondent housing association could provide any evidence of local authorities consistently, or indeed regularly, referring blind and partially sighted people for accommodation. Specialist associations reported that blind and partially sighted referrals were almost exclusively from

approved referral agencies (for example RNIB, Birmingham Royal Institute for the Blind, etc.).

Association respondents expressed the view that they expect this situation to continue for the foreseeable future, on the grounds that an increasing resource for capital programmes is coming through local authorities in terms of both land and money. This finding conforms with material gathered at the Corporation at its regional level.

In summary, the specific needs of blind and partially sighted people were not found to be reflected in local authority housing allocation practices; referrals and allocations were, at the time of the field work dominated by homeless and single parent families.

The Government has recently issued a consultation paper 'Access to Housing' (1) which suggests this 'fast track' approach is currently under review. We recommend that any new criteria introduced for the allocation of housing should take full account of the special needs of people with a visual impairment. See recommendation 9.3 (iv).

6.11   Homelessness

Part III of the Housing Act 1985 places a legal obligation on all local authorities in England and Wales to help people who are homeless or threatened with homelessness.

To satisfy the form of assistance given – temporary or permanent accommodation, or advice – local authorities investigate an applicant's circumstances and determine eligibility by applying the following tests:

- Is the applicant homeless or threatened with homelessness?

- Is the applicant in priority need?

- Is the applicant intentionally homeless?

and

- Does the applicant have a local connection?

To assist local authorities with the interpretation of the Act, the Department of Environment (DoE) published a Code of Guidance. It is not binding upon authorities, but authorities must have regard to it when discharging their responsibilities.

Neither the 1985 Housing Act, nor the Code of Guidance, refers specifically to visual (or sensory) impairment. The closest reference is physical disability under the test for 'vulnerability' (which is itself subsumed in the 'priority need' clause). However, people with a visual impairment can be in 'priority need' on account of pregnancy, living with dependent children, old age, or because they are expected to reside with someone who satisfies one of these conditions.

For single visually impaired people or childless visually impaired couples, the concept of vulnerability becomes of paramount importance when establishing whether they are entitled to re-housing. 'Vulnerable' means more than a waiting list medical priority. Paragraph 6.10 of the Code of Guidance states:

"The critical test when assessing vulnerability must be whether the applicant is less able to fend for him/herself so that s/he will suffer injury or detriment in circumstances, when a less vulnerable person would be able to cope without harmful effects".

Case law has also clarified the position. R v LB Lambeth ex p Carroll linked 'fending for oneself' to the ability of an applicant to find and keep accommodation. The difficulties of visually impaired people securing accommodation in both the private and public sector are well documented and therefore local authorities may rely on this precedent to accept people with visual impairments in 'priority need'.

Authorities have also set a visually impaired persons' 'priority need' status against a sliding scale of sight loss. In those authorities, a blind applicant is automatically regarded to be 'vulnerable' while, depending on the degree of vision and contributory factors, partially sighted applicants may not be considered so. Such practices are unsatisfactory.

This research indicates that all people with a registered or registerable visual impairment should be considered 'vulnerable' and we recommend this must be made explicit in a revised Code of Guidance or in local authorities homeless persons' policies.

6.12 Integration of Service – Collaboration between Agencies and Quality of Service

Overall, collaboration between agencies involved in identifying and meeting housing need (voluntary agencies, housing associations, local authorities and ultimately the Corporation) is inconsistent in character. A mixture of informal and formal mechanisms exist. There appears to be a considerable amount of informal day-to-day contact between officials, some respondents

reported more formalised arrangements, such as regular meetings.

Large associations reported a formalised approach with a structured agenda for meetings with local authorities every quarter. Similarly, some associations have sought to form 'partnerships' with social service departments and health authorities in order to identify and meet the special housing needs of people with mental health or mental handicap problems and learning difficulties.

There was, however, no evidence of formal or informal arrangements dedicated to identifying and meeting the housing needs of blind and partially sighted people. In summary, this group in the community was not perceived to have any particular housing needs beyond the general level of provision, except in the case of specialist agencies.

A systematic approach to housing needs assessment and provision across the span of agencies and organisations was thus difficult to find. The absence of basic information on the incidence of visual impairment and the daily living and housing needs of blind and partially sighted people is at the base of this situation and, in turn, frustrates efforts to identify and meet need across the span of housing providers.

6.13 Key Points Summarised

(i)   Housing Associations are heavily dependent on local authorities for information generally, and the setting of special needs priorities.

(ii)   Housing associations produce little primary information themselves, many operate administration and information procedures which are limited.

(iii)   At the time of the field work, generalist housing associations demonstrated at best minimal understanding of blind and partially sighted people and their housing needs. There was some evidence of an intuitive level of understanding, but no detailed in depth grasp, of for example design aspects.

(iv)   Blind and partially sighted people tend not to be perceived as priority group by housing associations, other than specialist operators.

(v)   Local authorities, as the key strategic agencies, tend to have poor quality information on blind and partially sighted people and their housing needs.

(vi)   Blind and partially sighted people are not identified specifically within priority needs categories in the homeless legislation.

(vii)   Current arrangements for identifying and meeting housing needs of visually impaired people are inefficient and fragmented.

(viii)   Collaboration and integration of services between key providers is undermined by a lack of reliable information, inconsistent communication mechanisms, and variable understanding of policy and priority setting mechanisms. The needs of blind and partially sighted people tend not to be described or fully understood, and are not perceived to be a priority.

7 Housing visually impaired people: access and design

7.1 Gaining Access to Housing

Section 3.8 of this report identified a range of general factors relating to blind and partially sighted people and their access to housing.

These range from the crucial importance of accessible information and advice concerning housing, through to mobility and environmental factors - transport, location, security. The Corporation's Housing Scheme Development Standards document does point to the relevance of some of these issues [1].

Information in appropriate formats, which is easy to access, is of critical importance to blind and partially sighted people who wish to find out about housing opportunities and possibilities. Similarly, advice, and particularly support, in searching for appropriate housing has been revealed by research carried out in connection with this and other studies as being of vital importance.

Many of the housing associations and other agencies contacted have well established equal opportunities policies. Few respondents participating in the research, however, were able to demonstrate a clear understanding of the importance of information and advice in relation to access to housing opportunities. Only specialist housing providers were able to provide information and advice in appropriate formats. There is as yet only one national source of housing information and advice, the RNIB Housing Information Service.

Blind and partially sighted people experience barriers caused by the absence of information on gaining access to the housing market. This is compounded by the fact that the majority of blind and partially sighted people of working age are on low incomes and have few savings and, therefore, have limited housing options. The overall consequence is that blind and partially sighted people often do not have the degree of opportunity, choice and self determination enjoyed by others.

The research, other studies and indeed experience gathered by a range of general information and housing providers demonstrates quite conclusively that blind and partially sighted people frequently encounter problems in getting access to systems of housing letting operated by local authorities and housing associations. Lack of information on the presence of blind and partially sighted people is at the base of this situation, which is compounded by inadequate understanding of their housing preferences and needs.

The provision of information on housing and how to access it, in a range of appropriate formats and, importantly, distributed effectively is crucially important. Without sound approaches to this, blind and partially sighted people will routinely encounter further barriers to access.

Frequently, absence of information is compounded by inefficiencies in communication and collaboration between housing funders and providers.

Further, the research has revealed few innovative or effective approaches to distribution of information to blind and partially sighted people, and communication generally. There was no evidence, for example, demonstrating communication with blind and partially sighted people by generalist housing associations through the extensive national network of organisations of and for blind people. These can be used with great effect to reach visually impaired people, seek their views and to disseminate information.

As part of the research, a review of currently published information on housing produced by housing and advice and information providers was undertaken. This element of the work was based on the ongoing work of RNIB's Housing Advice Service, which routinely reviews all publications and information material from housing providers.

The picture which emerges is not encouraging. There was found to be no evidence of housing advice and access material produced by generalist housing associations being made available in accessible formats. Some special needs providers produce limited information, usually of a very general and descriptive nature. Quantities produced tend to be very limited and all too frequently the quality of material, whether in large print, tactual or audio formats, is poor. It is rare for established communication channels used by blind and partially sighted people, such as talking newspapers or the network of organisations, to be used to disseminate information. It seems clear that scope for improvement in the information which enables access to housing and mechanisms used to disseminate it is considerable.

7.2 General Housing Design

Design aspects of housing for blind and partially sighted people was an area of focus in discussions with respondents contributing to the research.

Almost without exception, respondents having an involvement in the design and development of dwellings demonstrated little understanding of the specific design needs of blind and partially sighted people. Some respondents expressed the view that blind and partially sighted people generally are provided for by other organisations or did not have special (design) needs in the way that, for example, wheelchair users do.

Those respondents with a degree of awareness of the needs of blind and partially sighted people tended to demonstrate a limited knowledge, usually gained through the work of organisations, such as the Access Committee for England, which covers accessibility issues relating to buildings and public buildings.

Perhaps the most salient (and disturbing) point to emerge, however, was that many organisations involved in the provision of housing for elderly people appeared not to be aware that in later life nearly all elderly people are affected by physical changes affecting the lens of the eye and internal changes to the structure of the eye and muscles which surround and control the eye's movement. As a consequence of these changes, older people tend to experience increased difficulties in seeing, increased sensitivity to glare, blurred retinal images and increased difficulty associated with adapting vision when moving from areas of differential lighting levels or poorly laid out lighting. Such progressive vision degeneration is often and normally treatable by use of spectacles or low vision aids. This, however, is not always the case.

For many older people, these gradual changes in vision occur over a long period of time. As a consequence, many develop strategies for coping, particularly within communal or family surroundings. Many are reluctant to acknowledge that they may have a progressively deteriorating visual impairment.

There are design implications rooted in the above factors which affect many associations and generalist providers of housing to older people as well as providers of housing to blind and partially sighted people. Design considerations put in place for blind and partially sighted people are normally of great benefit to all older people.

If it is a basic aim of the social housing movement to produce housing appropriate for multi-generational living, logic suggests that design considerations appropriate to blind and partially sighted people should be an integral component of the design specifications of all or most housing.

7.3 Specific Design Aspects

Design considerations relating to blind and partially sighted people occur in the areas of lighting, signage, contrasting and colour co-ordination, textures and tactile coding, auditory identification aids, the elimination of hazards and sensible layout and use of space in relation to mobility considerations.

- Lighting design – Adequate lighting which exceeds current standards, allows visually impaired people to make the most of remaining vision. Light levels should be evenly distributed avoiding pools of light and dark. Up-lighters which bounce light off ceilings and walls producing glare should be avoided. Dimmer systems which allow for adjustment to suit individual eye conditions and needs are recommended. Good natural light is important, but glare should be controlled by the use of horizontal and vertical blinds, tinted and 'anti-glare' glass.

- Signage – Signage should be informative and effective to all users of housing. This may include signage in large print and the use of colour contrasts between characters and background surfaces. Tactile signs should always be embossed and not engraved.

- Contrast and colour-coding – Design should ensure that there is a good contrast between key surfaces within the home or building. Good contrast is required between walls and floor, background surfaces and fittings. Floors should have matt finishes which do not produce window or light fitting reflections. To maximise the light available it is advisable to use pale matt colours on walls. Heavily patterned floor and wall coverings should be avoided as they can cause visual confusion. Plugs, switches and guide-rails should all contrast with their background. Further attention to detail is required for some fittings to assist ease of use, for example, guide-rails should be between 40mm and 50mm in diameter and should be supported on brackets which do not obstruct continuous contact.

27

- Texture and tactile coding – Tactile surfaces can be used within buildings for way finding, as landmarks and to warn of hazards. On floors, this can include special profile flooring or simple changes in texture. Guide-rails should ideally incorporate tactile coding including raised markers denoting breaks in the rail and levels within the building. All doors should have tactile symbols which also contrast with door colour. Domestic machinery and equipment, including cookers and taps, should be identifiable tactually.

- Design of space and layout – Space within residencies should ideally be used so as to ensure ease of movement at all times. The threshold in all door ways should be flush. Where a weather bar is fitted on an external door, this should not exceed 15mm and have radiused edges. Internal side hung doors would ideally be 1000mm wide. Stairs should be straight wherever possible. If a change of direction is necessary this should be achieved by the use of a half landing, rather than by two or three steps. Steps on staircases should be uniformed with the treads not less than 280mm and the riser not greater than 150mm. The edge of each step should be highlighted with non-reflective, non-slip nosing. Risk of collision and injury must be avoided. Glazed doors and side panels should also be highlighted with prominent features and wall edges rounded were possible. Where obstructions are unavoidable they need to be appropriately highlighted using tactile and auditory clues.

Recommendations concerning design aspects appear in Section 9 of this report. Design aspects are dealt with in greater detail in the forthcoming RNIB Design Guide, which is recommended reading for all those developing housing facilities.

7.4 Key Points Summarised

(i) Access to housing via information in appropriate formats is crucially important. Without this, blind and partially sighted people's access to housing is adversely affected.

(ii) Housing design for blind and partially sighted people is frequently relevant to older people generally.

(iii) There are key special design areas relating to lighting, tactual coding, signage, design of housing and room layout.

8 Summary and Conclusions

8.1 Summary

This is the report of a study concerning the housing needs of blind and partially sighted people and the policies and practices for identifying and meeting these needs.

This report provides an overview of the numbers of blind and partially sighted in Great Britain and detailed estimates of numbers by Housing Corporation and local authority administrative units. Key indicators of the lifestyles of blind and partially sighted people are described.

An overview is provided of the strategies and policies which exist to identify housing needs and provide appropriate housing for blind and partially sighted people, systems of housing allocation are summarised. The main barriers affecting access to appropriate housing are identified, including the absence of basic information and a disjointed system of needs assessment and cross-agency collaboration and low levels of awareness of housing-related needs of visually impaired people.

8.2 Conclusions

(i) Blind and partially sighted people, numbers and lifestyle – there are approximately one million blind or partially sighted people in Great Britain. In addition, there are approximately 700,000 people who are not regarded as blind or partially sighted, but who have a visual impairment which means that they cannot recognise a friend across a road. The majority of blind and partially sighted people fall within the older age bands. Blind and partially sighted people tend to lead isolated lives and experience mobility problems. Access to information and awareness of opportunities is typically low. Blind and partially sighted people tend to have a lower income than other groups within the community, many also experience daily living problems, for example, with domestic and personal care tasks.

(ii) Identification of housing need – significant problems have been revealed concerning sources of information on blind and partially sighted people and their housing need. Until the recent RNIB Needs Survey and 1991 Census, official registration figures provided a substantial underestimate of the incidence of visual impairment. Information on housing need has been pinpointed as a particularly problematic area. Responsibilities for the collection of information, both on the numbers of blind and partially sighted people and their housing needs, nationally and locally, are not always clear. Information gathering practice varies considerably across the country and in its quality. As a direct consequence, assessment of needs, and allocation of housing is adversely affected to the detriment of this group in the community. Local authorities, as key housing strategy agencies, and housing associations, as key social housing providers, frequently lack the resources or incentives to address these problems. This, and other, research has revealed that policy, on which to base good practice, is inconsistent. The level of understanding of the detailed design issues relating to housing blind and partially sighted people has been shown to vary very considerably from agency to agency and region to region.

(iii) Information as a base for housing provision for blind and partially sighted people – procedures employed by local authorities, for the identification of visual impairment, are not effective. Housing associations are, in the main, reliant upon local authorities in terms of setting local housing strategy (which should incorporate special needs aspects) and, frequently, referral of people for accommodation. Thus, shortcomings in procedures employed by local authorities for identifying visual impairment and associated housing needs knock on to affect housing associations. Overall, there are limitations in the system(s) currently employed to determine housing policy, and thus provision which undermines fair access to housing by blind and partially sighted people.

(iv) Strategy for access to housing – evidence from this and other studies strongly suggests that visual impairment is not a factor which is directly taken into account in formulating local housing strategy, and allocation policies. Indeed, is not an issue which many housing staff regard as a priority or are aware of. Nationally, there are a few specialist Housing Associations which provide accommodation for blind and partially sighted people which take account of special design and environmental aspects. The research

29

reveals little evidence that local authority housing stock directly reflects visual impairment design aspects; similarly, generalist housing associations appear to make little provision for blind and partially sighted people in the form of appropriate design in new or existing schemes.

(v)   Design aspects – a range of general and environmental access issues relating to housing provision for blind and partially sighted people and are identified in this report. Similarly, a range of specific considerations relating to design aspects of housing for blind and partially sighted people are identified. These are, in the main, low-tech and low cost measures which could, and should, be incorporated into design of generic or mainstream housing under local authority or housing association management.

(vi)   Equal opportunities – housing organisations should differentiate sensory impairment from physical disability in their equal opportunities policy and practice. Such a move is required to heighten awareness of sensory impairment as a housing issue and tackle the homogenous view of disability and the association of disability with physical (wheelchair) handicap. Access to housing is primarily an equal opportunities issue. At present, blind and partially sighted people encounter barriers, both institutional and within policy and provision systems, in accessing housing. These frequently stem from inadequate information systems, inadequate awareness of housing needs of blind and partially sighted people and low priority being ascribed to this group in the community. Direct measures are required to address these shortcomings and provide blind and partially sighted people with fair access to housing opportunities.

9 Recommendations

9.1 Introduction

The recommendations below stem directly from the findings of this research. Recommendations are made as follows:

- To the Housing Corporation

- To Local Authorities

- To Housing Associations: Information and Media

- Housing Management and Good Practice Guidelines for Associations

- General Recommendations

The recommendations are relational, and are intended to form an integrated package, affecting provision of housing to people with a visual impairment by each agency and in an overall sense. The principal themes of the recommendations are:

- Information and management systems

- Monitoring of activity and performance

- Design aspects

- Training

- Housing management (good practice guidelines)

- The need for further research

9.2 Recommendations to the Housing Corporation

(i) Performance Standards for Housing Associations – April 1994 saw the introduction of the Corporation's new regulatory regime, known as 'Performance Review'. The process is supported by the guidance found in 'Performance Standards for Housing Associations' (1), which contains specific guidance on functional standards. Given the incidence of visual impairment documented in this report, and similarly the systemic barriers in accessing housing faced by visually impaired people, it is recommended that the Performance Standard guidance be amended to specifically refer to visually impaired people and their housing needs. This would build on the existing requirement to provide information in braille in the review of the Tenants'

Guarantee. Amendments are recommended in the guidance concerning access to housing and equal opportunities. Consideration should be given by the Corporation to a further amendment to its guidance concerning housing management and tenants with special needs.

(ii) Performance Review – this procedure is designed to support implementation of the new standards. It is recommended that the monitoring documentation and procedure for 1996/97 be amended to reflect the incidence and housing needs of visually impaired people.

Specifically, it is recommended that monitoring of the functional standards relating to equal opportunities and lettings includes questions in the numbers of lettings made to people with a sensory and/or visual impairment. Consideration should also be given to a further amendment to monitoring of the functional standard relating to tenants with special needs. Specifically, consideration should be given to the question covering the number of dwellings built during the year under management with characteristics specifically for, or incorporating features relevant to, visually impaired people, and the proportion of the total stock.

(iii) Scheme Development Standards – the Corporation should amend its Scheme Development Standards to incorporate good practice guidelines, designed to produce better practice amongst housing associations concerning blind and partially sighted people. Specific areas for guidance should include assessment, allocation, and design aspects. Design aspects relevant to blind and partially sighted people are normally relevant to other groups and should be incorporated into all new schemes (see Housing Management Recommendations).

(iv) Performance Indicators – the recent review of and amendments to the Corporation's Performance Audit Visit Manual improved reference to sensory impairment. Future reviews (which feed automatically through to performance indicators) should include development of indicators relevant to blind and partially sighted people as necessary.

(v) New stock for visually impaired people – it is recommended that the Corporation considers ways of making available resources for the development of housing opportunities for blind and partially sighted people at the *regional* and *sub-regional* levels, in partnership with housing associations, where it can be *demonstrated* that specific development and provision is appropriate. This would enable better provision where otherwise none would exist, in large part because of the thinly spread nature of the visually impaired population. The case for development would be dependent on quantification of this group at sub-regional level, and a detailed profiling of specific need, for example housing with care. This proposal is made recognising the underlying need to improve access to (appropriate) housing generally.

9.3 Recommendations to Local Authorities

(i) Information on incidence of visual impairment – The current Blind and Partially Sighted Register is an inadequate mechanism for quantifying the incidence of visual impairment. It is recommended that local authorities take steps under the community care planning programme to improve registration procedures with measures such as more effective collaboration between social service departments, family practitioners and optometrists. Additionally, it is recommended that local authorities adopt statistics on incidence within their boundaries prepared by the Office of Population, Census and Surveys and Royal National Institute for the Blind on the incidence of visual impairment as contained in this report.

(ii) Local housing need identification – procedures for identifying and assessing housing needs require improvement. It is recommended that local authorities:

(a) prioritise improvements to information systems employed by housing departments;

(b) increase investment in research and policy analysis concerning visual impairment and the housing, information and service needs of blind and partially sighted people;

(c) improve, and where necessary create, effective consultation

mechanisms as they relate to family health service authorities, local organisations and societies of/for blind and partially sighted people, voluntary and community groups in the wider sense and the housing associations.

(iii) Accessible media – information is absolutely crucial in facilitating access to housing. It is recommended that local authorities conduct a review of their information and documentation relating to housing to assess its appropriateness for blind and partially sighted people. Local authorities should adopt a policy of providing information on housing and housing opportunity in appropriate media, including tactual and audio media, making information available in a range of formats. This should apply particularly to information on housing and application documentation. Advice from organisations such as RNIB should be sought in this connection.

(iv) Assessment and allocations policy – visual impairment should be recognised as a criteria for priority allocation of housing. Policy relating to assessments and waiting lists should be amended accordingly, following consultation around the Government's Access to Housing' discussion paper. Assessment procedures should be reviewed and improved to ensure that the detailed housing needs aspects of blind or partially sighted people are effectively identified in order to ensure speedy and appropriate allocation of property, either by the local authority direct or via referral to a housing association.

(v) Training – in the housing needs of blind and partially sighted people should be a high priority in local authority housing departments. Staff in key positions, including allocations managers, stock managers and wardens, should receive such training as soon as possible. Advice from organisations such as RNIB should be sought in this connection.

(vi) Good practice guidelines – local authority housing departments should, as a matter of urgency, develop good practice guidelines relating to sensory impairment and specifically the housing needs of blind and partially sighted people. Advice from organisations such as RNIB should be sought in this connection.

(vii) Tenant consultation and participation – formal consultation mechanisms should be enhanced and established to ensure that full account is taken in management and policy development of the housing needs of blind and partially sighted people.

(viii) Local housing strategy – local authorities should demonstrate full and effective consideration of the housing needs of blind and partially sighted people in their housing strategies. Performance indicators should be used to reflect this.

9.4 Recommendations to Housing Associations: Information and Media

(i) Information systems – information is the life blood of any service delivery agency. Evidence indicates that there is scope for improvement in basic information, documentation and administrative systems in housing associations. Specifically, the registering and analysis of enquiries is an area that should be improved. Accordingly, it is recommended that improvements to information systems be developed under guidance from the Housing Corporation and the National Federation of Housing Associations (NFHA). Performance indicators relating to information systems and administrative standards should be developed by NFHA, and gathered as part of improved monitoring by the Corporation.

(ii) Documentation – guidelines and, where appropriate, standardised documentation should be developed for use within housing associations to ensure good practice concerning housing needs of blind and partially sighted people.

9.5 Housing Management Good Practice Guidelines for Associations

Development of management guidelines designed to facilitate fair access to appropriate housing for visually impaired people is a vital next step.

(i) Information provision and access – housing providers should be guided by a clear policy on access to information for blind and partially sighted people. This should offer the capacity to provide information in media that are appropriate to them, that is, large print, audio tape cassette, ordinary print in the appropriate typeface or braille on request. Examples of

information and documentation that should be provided in accessible media are:-

■ Promotional material

■ Applications forms

■ Tenancy agreements

■ Rent notification letters

■ Tenants' handbook and tenants' association information

■ Repairs notification forms

■ All legal documents

■ Complaints procedures

■ Equal opportunities policies

■ Allocation policies

■ Newsletters

(ii) Marketing and promotional policy – this should be established by housing providers. It should seek to ensure that visually impaired and other disabled people are reached by promotional material. Only a quarter of visually impaired people are registered, so other strategies must be developed which do not first rely on social services departments.

(iii) An equal opportunities policy – which covers employment and service delivery issues with regard to people with a visual impairment should be implemented. This policy should differentiate between physical and sensory impairments, because some of the needs that have to be met are so different. Any policy statement should be backed up with a programme of implementation of points from this good practice guide. Housing organisations, offices, particularly reception areas, should be accessible to all disabled people, and this means that the particular needs of sensory impaired people should be considered as well as those of persons in wheelchairs. Accessibility is not only about design features, it is also about the attitudes and awareness that underpin behaviour and procedures.

(iv) Physical access – to housing organisation offices, particularly reception areas, should be enabled through appropriate design.

(v) Open access to housing – a positive commitment to empower people with a visual impairment with regard to accessing housing provision and officers within the organisation should permeate the organisation's operation.

Given the difficulties in reaching visually impaired people, housing providers should consider granting *referral and nomination rights* to bona fide organisations of people with a visual impairment. Accessibility is not only about procedural and design features, it is also about the attitudes and awareness that underpin behaviour and procedures.

Integrated waiting lists within geographical areas can be useful if they are used positively, but some discretion should be used to protect all categories of persons to ensure a fair distribution of vacancies.

(vi) Application forms – should seek effectively to ascertain the needs of the applicant. To aid this process and to aid effective monitoring, a question should be included in the application form, for example:-

> Our housing association is positively committed to assisting people with disabilities –
>
> Do you have a sight problem?.....
>
> Are you registered disabled?.....
>
> We may need to contact you further on these points to see how we can help you.

(vii) A monitoring process – should be in place, which at all stages from application through to letting of a property, has a specific indicator for a tenant with visual impairment. This will enable effective performance monitoring once visually impaired applicants have been identified.

(viii) Housing allocation policies – should be vetted to ensure that they do not discriminate against people with a visual impairment.

(a) Many organisations do not have a list of properties which are suitable for people with disabilities. A review of housing stock to identify such

properties and potential properties would be a useful exercise. Failing a thorough review, void inspections should, amongst other issues, seek to return a verdict on the suitability of the property for disabled people.

(b) Visually impaired people should be encouraged to specify their requirements with regard to accommodation and support as their requirements will vary greatly.

(c) *Location of accommodation* is highly significant for people with a visually impairment, because of their need to use appropriate public transport, and their need for easy access to shopping and service facilities. This factor should be given some weight in allocating accommodation.

(d) Some discretion should be exercised on time to view when a property is offered to a visually impaired person as there may be difficulties in arranging transport, arranging a sighted guide, and so on. To speed this process, assisted viewing by one of the housing provider's officers should be considered and may be useful in establishing future rapport.

(e) Employment opportunities for visually impaired people are few and far between. Some consideration should be given to waiving *qualifying periods of residence* within particular localities where visually impaired people are in receipt of an offer of employment.

(f) *Security* both in personal terms and in terms of the appropriateness of the building design are important issues to people with a visual impairment. Some consideration for these issues should be given when allocating properties.

(ix) Letting policies

(a) 'No pets' rules should be waived with regard to people with a visual impairment who need a guide dog for mobility purposes. Toileting facilities for guide dogs may be a problem, but the Guide Dogs for the Blind Association can advise on this matter, and, have, on occasion given grants to assist with creation of a dog run or dog loo.

(b)   Braille users may have greater shelf and storage requirements than other people.

(c)   People with a visual impairment may require *assistance in getting services connected* when taking up a tenancy, and managers of that property should assist in getting service providers to *bill the tenant in the appropriate medium* to avoid financial confusion in the future.

(d)   Prior to the letting or subsequent to the letting, *formal liaison* with social services departments' occupational therapists should occur, particularly where there is a need for *disabled facility grant* to meet lighting or other design considerations.

(x)   Design guidelines and briefs – should include all of the issues that are relevant with regard to people with a visual impairment, particularly in schemes or areas where there is likely to be a concentration of older people. RNIB is currently in the process of publishing a design guide manual.

(xi)   Training in visual disability awareness – should be supplied to all appropriate housing staff. The training should not only cover the effects of various eye conditions, but should include a positive review of the interpersonal, organisational, design, and liaison issues with regard to the role of housing providers in meeting the needs of people with a visual impairment.

Further training in the area of *benefits/ grants available* for visually impaired people should be considered for those staff involved in adaptive and refurbishment work, debt counselling, and rent arrears recovery.

(xii)   Advice and the allocation – of accommodation to people with a visual impairment by housing providers should be done without charge.

(xiii)   Repairs and maintenance issues – should be dealt with in such a way as not to disadvantage people with a visual impairment. Those performing repair work should have their attention drawn to the needs of people with a visual impairment, particularly with regard to the need to avoid trailing wires, and other health and safety issues. Some thought needs to be given to this area. For example, visually impaired people cannot see "wet paint" signs. Some manufacturers now supply talking signs, and hazard bleeping audio boxes are available from RNIB.

People with a visual impairment cannot necessarily notice repairs and maintenance problems to notify to their Estate Manager. Some arrangements for helping inspection may therefore, need to be made.

(xiv)   Performance expectations – with regard to the number of visually impaired people to be housed, within certain time scales, and with regard to the quality of service to be delivered to those individuals should be set by housing providers.

(xv)   Allocations – allocation procedures should be monitored on an ongoing basis to ensure that blind and partially sighted people receive fair access to housing. The CORE procedure facilitates this.

(xvi)   Training – key staff in associations should receive training in sensory impairment and specifically the housing needs of blind and partially sighted people in order to raise awareness of these issues.

(xvii)   Design – associations should incorporate design features relevant to blind and partially sighted people in all new build schemes and, as appropriate, adaptations and improvements. The Housing Corporation should scrutinise implementation of this recommendation through an improved monitoring procedure.

(xviii)   Tenant participation – formalised tenant participation and consultative mechanisms should be established under guidelines from the Corporation and National Federation of Housing Associations. Amendments should be made to the Corporation Good Practice Guide and Performance Audit Visit Manual.

9.6   General Recommendations

(i)   Further research: blind and partially sighted people's experience of the housing market – beyond this study, which has provided an overview, a survey should be commissioned and carried out investigating, in further detail, blind and partially sighted people's experience of the housing market, their awareness of the structure of, and awareness of, opportunities within this market and their attitudes to special needs and design issues. Such a study may be undertaken or commissioned by an organisation representing visually impaired people, and should also include investigation of the housing-related aspirations of blind and partially sighted community.

(ii)   Further research: the work of housing associations and sensorily impaired people – beyond this study, which has provided an overview, a further survey should be carried out investigating housing associations' awareness of sensory impairment and special housing needs of sensorily impaired people. Specifically, such a survey should investigate, in further detail, assessment and allocations procedures and housing associations' awareness and use of equal opportunities principles.

(iii) CORE monitoring – the Housing Corporation should extend the CORE package to monitor new lettings to people with a sensory impairment as soon as is practicable. Guidelines on the new indicator(s) should be produced.

(iv)   Awareness of housing needs of blind and partially sighted people – organisations of and for blind and partially sighted people should improve their communications and awareness raising activities to ensure that awareness of the housing needs of blind and partially sighted people is raised and that they have a higher priority in formulation of local housing strategies. The RNIB should collaborate with appropriate agencies, including the NFHA to this effect.

(v)   Training resources – should be further developed and improved as a matter of priority by agencies, including the RNIB, for application by agreement with local authorities and housing associations.

Notes and Sources Appendix 1

Section 3:

(1)   Department of Health, *Registered Blind and Partially Sighted People at 31 March 1991, England,* GSS, HMSO, London, 1992

(2)   Bruce I, McKennell A, Walker E, *Blind and Partially Sighted Adults in Great Britain: The RNIB Survey,* HMSO, London, 1991

(3)   IBID. (Page 43)

(4)   Office of Population Census and Surveys: *Provisional 1991 Mid-Year Estimates, England and Wales, County Districts,* OPCS, London, 1991

(5)   Royal National Institute for the Blind: *Initial Demographic Study 1985 – A Review of Available Data on the Visually Disabled Population,* RNIB, London, 1986.

(6)   Shore, Penelope: *Local Authority Services for the Visually Impaired,* RNIB, London, 1989.

(7)   Bruce I, McKennell A, Walker E, *Blind and Partially Sighted Adults in Great Britain: The RNIB Survey,* HMSO, London, 1991 (Page 44)

(8)   IBID. (Page 151)

(9)   IBID. (Page 45)

(10)   IBID. (Page 170)

(11)   IBID. (Page 178)

(12)   IBID. (Page 169)

(13)   IBID. (Page 198)

(14)   IBID. (Page 135)

(15)   IBID. (Page 253)

(16)   IBID. (Page 49)

(17)   IBID. (Page 60)

Section 4:

(1)   The Gift of Thomas Pocklington, 20 Lansdowne Road, London W11 3LL. A charitable foundation which provides accommodation for blind and partially sighted people in residential care homes, sheltered flats and independent housing.

(2)   RNIB Housing Advocacy and Advice Service provides information and advice to blind and partially sighted people on housing matters. All enquiries are monitored, classified and entered onto a database. The data quoted relate to calendar year 1993 and is reported internally in the form of service indicator reports.

Section 6:

(1)   The Department of the Environment, *Access to Local Authority and Housing Association Tenancies – A Consultation Paper,* London, 1994.

Section 7:

[1]   The Housing Corporation *Scheme Development Standards,* Housing Corporation, London, 1993

Section 9:

[1]   The Housing Corporation *Performance Standards for Housing Associations,* Housing Corporation, London, 1994.

Research samples

Appendix 2(i)Research Respondents – Housing Corporation

Regional Offices

- Area Manager, London and Home Counties (North East)

- Area Manager, London and Home Counties (North West)

- Regional Director, London and Home Counties (South)

- Technical Officer, West

- Operations Manager, East Midlands

- Areas Manager, East Midlands

- Regional Director, West Midlands

- Area manager, West Midlands

- Operations Manager, North East

- Regional Director, North West

- Operations Manager, Merseyside

Headquarters

- Research Manager, Housing Management and Research Division

Appendix 2(ii): Research respondents – National Federation of Housing Associations

- Special Needs Manager

- Policy Adviser, Housing Care and Support

- Development Policy Officer, Housing Services and Research Division

Appendix 2(iii) Research respondents – housing associations

- North British Housing Association: Assistant Director

- London and Quadrant Housing Trust: Partnership Finance Coordinator Agency Coordinator

- Notting Hill Housing Trust: Director of Support and Short Stay Housing

- Carib Housing Association: Chairman Housing Officer

- Octavia Hill Housing Trust: Special Projects Officer

- Knightstone Housing Association: Housing Central Services Manager

- Bristol Churches Housing Association: Director of Housing Special Needs Assistant

- Leeds Federated Housing Association: Director of Housing

- Harewood Housing Society Ltd: Director of Housing

- Housemartin Housing Association: Area Team Managers

- Henshaw's Society for the Blind Housing Association: Director of Residential Services

- Carr-Gomm Society Ltd: Director

Appendix 2(iv): Research respondents – local authorities

RNIB's Housing Services maintain regular contact with personnel in many local authority housing and technical service departments, and counterparts in social service departments. In connection specifically with this research, the following housing departments were contacted and consulted:-

- London Borough of Camden

- London Borough of Hackney

- London Borough of Islington

- London Borough of Lambeth

- London Borough of Brent

- London Borough of Croydon

- London Borough of Ealing

- London Borough of Merton

- Royal Borough of Kensington and Chelsea

- Westminster City Council

- Poole Borough Council

- Bournemouth Borough Council

- Bristol City Council

- Leeds City Council

- Bradford City Council

- Manchester City Council

Appendix 2 (v): Interview schedule.

Housing Needs of Visually Impaired People.
RNIB research on behalf of the Housing
Corporation.
Core and agency specific interview questions for
Housing Corporation Regional Officers and
Housing Association representatives.

Section 1 *Structure of the organisation &
individual roles.*

1.1 Name:

1.2 Position in organisation:

1.3 Summary of role & principle responsibilities:

1.4 Outline the work of the Association/Region:

1.5 **H.A.** Does the organisation work with specific
client groups? e.g. elderly or single homeless?

1.6 How has the agency changed over the last five
years in either the way it works or who it works
with?
Probe: Have there been.......
i Changes in priorities
ii Changes in client group
iii Changes in funding

Section 2 *Information sources in general.*

2.1 What are your main sources of information on
housing need?
Probe: Do you gather information through........
i Research
ii Local authority housing departments
iii Local authority social service departments
iv Monitoring waiting lists
v Requests /enquiries.
vi # Housing associations

2.2 How do you gather this information on housing
need?
Probe: Does it come through........
i Formal networks
ii Informal networks
iii Commissioned projects
iv Established monitoring procedures.

2.3 How do you use this information?.
Probe: Does information on need..........
i To link in with policy development. (To be
covered in detail in section 5)
ii Influence priority setting.
iii # Inform funding decisions
iv Not get used in any formal sense.

2.4 Do you have sources of information on visual impairment and the needs of people with a visual impairment?
If so,
i What are these sources.
i i Have they in any way influenced the work of the association/region?

2.5 Who in your opinion should be responsible for gathering information on housing need?

Section 3 *Problems with information.*

3.1 What would you consider to be the main problems with information on housing need?

3.2 Is there a problem with consistency of information?

3.3 Is there a problem with gaining access to information?

3.4 Is there a problem with the credibility of the available information.?

Section 4 *Management practice and policy development.*

4.1 How are policies developed within the Association/Region?
Probe: Are policies set........
i By committee?
ii By officers?
iii Formally?
iv Informally?

4.2 How are priorities identified?
Probe: Does this tend to be......
i Through formal or informal procedures?

4.3 In what way does the region/association liaise with local authority housing departments with regard to housing provision and need identification?
Probe...
i. Does communication tend to be through formal or informal networks?
ii. How does information on housing need from the local authorities influence policy decisions?
iii. *HASH* How much variation is there in degree of consultation/communication that takes place between the regional office and various local authorities?

4.4 **H.C.** In what way does the region liaise with housing associations with regard to housing provision and need identification?
Probe....
i. Does communication tend to be through formal or informal networks?
ii. How does the information from the housing associations influence policy decisions?
iii. How much variation is there in the degree of consultation/communication that takes place between the regional office and the various housing associations?

4.5 How is information on housing need incorporated into policy making and priority setting & # funding?

4.6 **H.A.** Are the views of tenants represented in the policy making process?
If so,
i I low is participation made possible?

4.7 Does the association/region have a policy which relates to visually impaired people?
If so:
i What is the policy ?
ii How is it interpreted?

4.8 The Housing Corporation outlines 11 groups of tenants with special needs: (1 people with physical disability, 2 people with learning difficulties, 3 people with mental health problems, 4 people with drugs & alcohol problems, 5 people leaving penal establishments, 6 refugees, 7 people with AIDS or HIV, 8 Young people at risk or leaving care, 9 vulnerable women with children, 10 women at risk of domestic violence, 11 frail elderly.)

Which are the priority groups for your agency?

Section 5 *The link between information and practice.*

5.1 **H.C. (h.q.)** Can you outline how the housing needs indicator (H.N.I) is complied?

5.2 **H.C. (h.q.)** Would the needs of visually impaired people show up on the HNI?

5.3 **H.C.** How do you use the H.N.I in the formulation of local policy?

5.4 **H.C.** What would you say are the drawbacks to using the housing needs indicator?

5.5 **H.C.** Do the core indicators influence work in the region in respect to.....:
i Funding decisions
ii Monitoring
iii Provision
If yes, does this apply to homes for visually impaired people

5.6 **H.C.** On what basis are schemes funded?

5.7 **H.C.** How many schemes for sensory impaired people have been constructed in the last ten years?
If schemes have been funded probe:
i When was the scheme set up?
ii Why, and on what basis was the particular scheme funded?
iii Has the scheme been evaluated? If so,
iv What where the outcomes of the evaluation?

5.8 **H.C.** How much funding has gone into schemes for sensory impaired people in the last ten years?

5.9 **H.A.** How are properties allocated?

5.10 **H.A.** How many visually impaired tenants are in your accommodation?

5.11 **H.A.** Are your waiting lists 'open' or 'closed'?
If closed,
i For how long have the waiting lists been closed?
ii What is the main reason for the waiting lists being closed.?

5.12 **H.A.** Do you in any way monitor your waiting lists?
If so,
i Do you gather information on special needs?
ii Would sensory impairment be included with 'physical disability' in a category of it's own within special needs or within general needs housing?
iii How may visually impaired people are there on your waiting list?

5.13 **H.A.** Do you participate in gathering CORE indicator information on new lettings for the NFHA?
If so:
i Do the core indicators shape new forms of funding decisions?
ii Do the core indicators influence monitoring?
iii Do the core indicators effect provision of homes for Visually impaired people?

5.14 **H.A.** Do you monitor requests for advice and enquiries on housing issues?
If so,
i Have you received requests from visually impaired people regarding housing issues?

Section 6 *Visual impairment & equal opportunity issues.*

6.1 Does training for housing officers refer to good practice in relation to older people and sensory impairment?
If so:
i Who provides the training?
ii What form does it take?

6.2 Does the Association/corporation have any input or recommendations on design of homes?
If so:
i What form does this take?
ii Is there a designated officer or forum?
iii Does it include the design of accommodation for people with a sensory impairment?

6.3 **H.A.** In what way are user/tenants views represented in the association?

6.4 **H.A.** Are there any mechanisms set up to gather the views of visually impaired tenants?
Probe:
i Is information provided in an appropriate medium to their needs?

6.5 Are you aware of the number of visually impaired people in the region/within your area?
If so,
i How many visually impaired people are there in the region/ within your area.

6.6 What in your opinion are the housing needs of visually impaired people?

6.7 How in your opinion might the housing needs of visually impaired people go beyond that provided by general needs housing?.

6.8 To what extent is access to housing by visually impaired people perceived as......
i An equal opportunities issue?
ii An issues concerning adapted provision?

6.9 What in your opinion could be done to ensure that adequate provision for the needs of visually impaired people are encouraged?
Probe ....
i What could be done specifically by your agency?

Appendix 3(i)

Table 4.   The size of the Blind and Partially Sighted Population by Housing Corporation Region.[1]

Housing Corporation Region	Total Population[2]	Estimated Number of Visually Impaired People[3]
London & Home Counties South	**6,679,400**	**130,630**
Kent	1,536,100	29,090
East Sussex	715,600	19,420
West Sussex	712,300	17,440
Surrey	1,033,600	19,700
London Boroughs	2,681,800	44,980
London and Home Countles North East	**4,136,900**	**69,680**
Bedfordshire	532,400	7,880
Essex	1,547,000	28,280
London Boroughs	2,057,500	33,520
London and Home Counties North West	**3,778,600**	**62,080**
Buckinghamshire	639,100	9,450
Hertfordshire	988,600	16,490
London Boroughs	2,150,900	36,140
West	**7,757,900**	**151,780**
Avon	964,900	18,290
Berkshire	752,900	11,020
Cornwall	472,100	10,400
Devon	1,038,800	23,970
Dorset	660,600	16,980
Gloucestershire	539,300	10,390
Hampshire	1,581,800	27,940
Isle of White	126,400	3,310
Oxfordshire	580,900	9,440
Somerset	468,400	10,040
Wiltshire	571,800	10,000
East Midlands	**6,117,100**	**111,200**
Cambridgeshire	668,700	11,000
Derbyshire	943,200	16,990
Leicestershire	894,300	15,130
Lincolnshire	591,100	1 1,610
Norfolk	759,400	16,170
Northamptonshire	586,500	9,730
Nottinghamshire	1,020,200	17,670
Suffolk	653,700	12,900
West Midlands	**5,265,300**	**89,840**
Hereford & Worcestershire	685,400	12,490
Shropshire	411,600	7,210
Staffordshire	1,049,700	16,890
Warwickshire	489,200	8,520
West Midlands	2,629,400	44,730

Housing Corporation Region	Total Population[2]	Estimated Number of Visually Impaired People[3]
North East	**7,585,300**	**134,260**
Cleveland	559,700	8,480
Durham	605,700	10,580
Humberside	877,400	15,750
Northumberland	306,600	5,670
Tyne & Wear	1,130,400	19,980
Yorkshire	4,105,500	73,800
Merseyside	**1,950,700**	**33,860**
Merseyside	1,950,700	33,860
North West	**4,934,600**	**89,550**
Cheshire	574,500	10,320
Cumbria	489,200	9,420
Greater Manchester	2,570,600	44,320
Lancashire	1,300,300	25,490
TOTAL ENGLAND	**48,205,800**	**872,880**

[1]   Technical notes:

    (i)   The visually impaired population of GB comprises approximately 1.8% of the total population.

    (ii)   Evidence of geographical variance: There is currently no empirical evidence to suggest any geographical variation in incidence of visual impairment. Prevalence rates are ages related (see Fig 1), areas with a higher proportion of elderly people will as a consequence have higher incidence of visual impairment.

[2]   OPCS 1991 Mid year estimates for England. All figures for the general population have been rounded to the nearest 100

[3]   Unpublished figures based on prevalence rates identified in Blind and partially sighted adults in Britain: the RNIB survey Vol.1, by Ian Bruce, Aubrey McKennell and Errol Walker. HMSO, London, 1991. All RNIB population estimates for blind and partially sighted people have been rounded to the nearest 10

Table 5 (i) **The blind and partially sighted population of England by local authority administrative unit.
London and Home Counties (South) Region**

	Total Population	Estimated B & PS Population
KENT		
ASHFORD	93,500	1,700
CANTERBURY	130,300	3,120
DARTFORD	81,000	1,320
DOVER	105,400	2,220
GILLINGHAM	96,400	1,400
GRAVESHAM	93,600	1,500
MAIDSTONE	137,500	2,360
ROCHESTER UPON MEDWAY	147,000	2,060
SEVENOAKS	109,500	1,970
SHEPWAY	93,600	2,330
SWALE	116,900	1,980
THANET	126,900	3,430
TONBRIDGE & MALLING	102,500	1,620
TUNBRIDGE WELLS	102,000	2,080
KENT TOTAL	**1,536,100**	**29,090**
EAST SUSSEX		
BRIGHTON	154,200	3,280
EASTBOURNE	84,900	2,830
HASTINGS	83,400	2,060
HOVE	89,700	2,660
LEWES	88,600	2,300
ROTHER	83,100	2,920
WEALDEN	131,700	3,370
EAST SUSSEX TOTAL	**715,600**	**19,420**
WEST SUSSEX		
ADUR	58,900	1,490
ARUN	131,300	4,220
CHICHESTER	102,400	2,700
CRAWLEY	88,700	1,220
HORSHAM	110,300	2,210
MID SUSSEX	122,600	2,340
WORTHING	98,100	3,260
WEST SUSSEX TOTAL	**712,300**	**17,440**

	Total Population	Estimated B & PS Population
SURREY		
ELMBRIDGE	114,500	2,300
EPSOM & EWELL	67,900	1,490
GUILDFORD	126,500	2,270
MOLE VALLEY	79,600	1,760
REIGATE & BANSTEAD	118,700	2,380
RUNNYMEDE	74,700	1,370
SPELTHORNE	91,200	1,550
SURREY HEATH	80,000	1,080
TANDRIDGE	77,300	1,510
WAVERLEY	116,100	2,500
WOKING	87,100	1,490
SURREY TOTAL	**1,033,600**	**19,700**
LONDON BOROUGHS		
BEXLEY	219,400	3,770
BROMLEY	294,700	5,670
CROYDON	319,200	5,200
GREENWICH	213,600	3,640
KINGSTON UPON THAMES	137,500	2,610
LAMBETH	256,600	2,440
LEWISHAM	240,800	4,010
MERTON	171,800	3,180
RICHMOND UPON THAMES	164,300	3,300
SOUTHWARK	227,200	3,540
SUTTON	171,400	3,290
WANDSWORTH	265,300	4,330
LONDON BOROUGHS TOTAL	**2,681,800**	**44,980**
TOTAL LONDON AND HOME COUNTIES (SOUTH)	**6,679,400**	**130,630**

Table 5 (ii)   The blind and partially sighted population of England by local authority administrative unit. London and Home Counties (North East) Region

	Total Population	Estimated B & PS Population
BEDFORDSHIRE		
NORTH BEDFORDSHIRE	136,200	2,270
LUTON	174,600	2,400
MID BEDFORDSHIRE	111,800	1,660
SOUTH BEDFORDSHIRE	109,800	1,550
BEDFORDSHIRE TOTAL	**532,400**	**7,880**
ESSEX		
BASILDON	162,700	2,350
BRAINTREE	119,800	2,120
BRENTWOOD	70,800	1,300
CASTLE POINT	87,100	1,400
CHELMSFORD	154,100	2,380
COLCHESTER	145,900	2,500
EPPING FOREST	117,000	2,200
HARLOW	75,600	1,030
MALDON	52,900	940
ROCHFORD	75,800	1,340
SOUTHEND-ON-SEA	162,500	3,990
TENDRING	127,100	3,790
THURROCK	129,600	1,810
UTTLESFORD	66,100	1,130
ESSEX TOTAL	**1,547,000**	**28,280**
LONDON BOROUGHS		
CITY OF LONDON	4,100	60
BARKING & DAGENHAM	146,200	2,770
ENFIELD	263,200	4,780
HACKNEY	187,900	2,660
HARINGEY	211,800	3,020
HAVERING	232,500	3,950
ISLINGTON	173,500	2,630
NEWHAM	221,300	3,080
REDBRIDGE	231,200	4,280
TOWER HAMLETS	168,100	2,420
WALTHAM FOREST	217,700	3,870
LONDON BOROUGHS TOTAL	**2,057,500**	**33,520**
TOTAL LONDON AND HOME COUNTIES (NORTH EAST)	**4,136,900**	**69,680**

Table 5 (iii)   The blind and partially sighted population of England by local authority administrative unit. London and Home Counties (North West) Region

	Total Population	Estimated B & PS Population
BUCKINGHAMSHIRE		
AYLESBURY VALE	148,000	2,160
SOUTH BUCKINGHAMSHIRE	62,400	1,170
CHILTERN	89,700	1,600
MILTON KEYNES	179,200	2,130
WYCOMBE	159,800	2,390
BUCKINGHAMSHIRE TOTAL	**639,100**	**9,450**
HERTFORDSHIRE		
BROXBOURNE	82,300	1,210
DACORUM	134,000	2,130
EAST HERTFORDSHIRE	117,800	1,820
HERTSMERE	88,800	1,670
NORTH HERTFORDSHIRE	113,000	2,020
ST ALBANS	126,700	2,160
STEVENAGE	76,200	1,030
THREE RIVERS	79,300	1,490
WATFORD	75,500	1,260
WELWYN HATFIELD	95,000	1,700
HERTFORDSHIRE TOTAL	**988,600**	**16,490**
LONDON BOROUGHS		
BARNET	299,900	5,840
BRENT	248,600	3,630
CAMDEN	181,700	3,140
EALING	281,800	4,430
HAMMERSMITH & FULHAM	156,200	2,430
HARROW	203,800	3,790
HILLINGDON	236,800	4,040
HOUNSLOW	209,100	3,290
KENSINGTON & CHELSEA	145,300	2,280
CITY OF WESTMINSTER	187,700	3,270
LONDON BOROUGHS TOTAL	**2,150,900**	**36,140**
TOTAL LONDON AND HOME COUNTIES (NORTH WEST)	**3,778,600**	**62,080**

Table 5 (iv)   The blind and partially sighted population of England by local authority administrative unit. West Region

	Total Population	Estimated B & PS Population
AVON		
BATH	84,100	1,900
BRISTOL	397,000	7,460
KINGSWOOD	90,500	1,500
NORTHAVON	132,700	1,870
WANSDYKE	80,800	1,560
WOODSPRING	179,800	4,000
AVON TOTAL	**964,900**	**18,290**
BERKSHIRE		
BRACKNELL FOREST	98,800	1,260
NEWBURY	139,300	2,060
READING	136,200	2,200
SLOUGH	102,400	1,450
WINDSOR & MAIDENHEAD	134,200	2,290
WOKINGHAM	142,000	1,760
BERKSHIRE TOTAL	**752,900**	**11,020**
CORNWALL		
CARADON	78,100	1,580
CARRICK	83,800	2,000
KERRIER	88,700	1,840
NORTH CORNWALL	74,300	1,680
PENWITH	59,900	1,430
RESTORMEL	87,300	1,870
CORNWALL TOTAL	**472,100**	**10,400**
DEVON		
EAST DEVON	118,100	3,720
EXETER	105,400	2,040
NORTH DEVON	85,500	1,960
PLYMOUTH	254,400	4,470
SOUTH HAMS	78,400	1,800
TEIGNBRIDGE	110,000	2,840
MID DEVON	65,100	1,350
TORBAY	122,600	3,550
TORRIDGE	53,100	1,190
WEST DEVON	46,200	1,050
DEVON TOTAL	**1,038,800**	**23,970**

	Total Population	Estimated B & PS Population
DORSET		
BOURNEMOUTH	158,800	4,590
CHRISTCHURCH	41,200	1,390
NORTH DORSET	53,800	1,250
POOLE	135,100	3,140
PURBECK	43,500	980
WEST DORSET	86,900	2,270
WEYMOUTH & PORTLAND	62,200	1,300
EAST DORSET	79,100	2,060
DORSET TOTAL	**660,600**	**16,980**
GLOUCESTERSHIRE		
CHELTENHAM	108,100	2,180
COTSWOLD	75,100	1,680
FOREST OF DEAN	75,900	1,430
GLOUCESTER	104,700	1,720
STROUD	104,400	2,060
TEWKESBURY	71,100	1,320
GLOUCESTERSHIRE TOTAL	**539,300**	**10,390**
HAMPSHIRE		
BASINGSTOKE & DEANE	146,000	1,990
EAST HAMPSHIRE	104,100	1,830
EASTLEIGH	106,900	1,650
FAREHAM	99,800	1,740
GOSPORT	76,600	1,310
HART	80,900	1,100
HAVANT	120,300	2,100
NEW FOREST	161,800	3,950
PORTSMOUTH	188,800	3,710
RUSHMOOR	86,800	1,170
SOUTHAMPTON	207,300	3,760
TEST VALLEY	103,900	1,670
WINCHESTER	98,600	1,960
HAMPSHIRE TOTAL	**1,581,800**	**27,940**
ISLE OF WIGHT		
MEDINA	72,000	1,720
SOUTH WIGHT	54,400	1,590
ISLE OF WIGHT TOTAL	**126,400**	**3,310**

	Total Population	Estimated B & PS Population
OXFORDSHIRE		
CHERWELL	125,000	1,810
OXFORD	130,300	2,250
SOUTH OXFORDSHIRE	120,700	2,060
VALE OF WHITE HORSE	112,900	1,790
WEST OXFORDSHIRE	92,000	1,530
OXFORDSHIRE TOTAL	**580,900**	**9,440**
SOMERSET		
MENDIP	97,800	1,890
SEDGEMOOR	99,300	2,080
TAUNTON DEANE	95,800	2,040
WEST SOMERSET	32,100	960
SOUTH SOMERSET	143,400	3,070
SOMERSET TOTAL	**468,400**	**10,040**
WILTSHIRE		
KENNET	69,700	1,300
NORTH WILTSHIRE	113,800	1,930
SALISBURY	106,600	2,160
THAMESDOWN	172,900	2,550
WEST WILTSHIRE	108,800	2,060
WILTSHIRE TOTAL	**571,800**	**10,000**
TOTAL WEST	**7,757,900**	**151,780**

Table 5 (v)   The blind and partially sighted population of England by local authority administrative unit. East Midlands Region

	Total Population	Estimated B & PS Population
CAMBRIDGESHIRE		
CAMBRIDGE	108,000	1,920
EAST CAMBRIDGESHIRE	61,200	1,150
FENLAND	75,500	1,490
HUNTINGDONSHIRE	146,500	2,060
PETERBOROUGH	155,000	2,350
SOUTH CAMBRIDGESHIRE	122,500	2,030
CAMBRIDGESHIRE TOTAL	**668,700**	**11,000**
DERBYSHIRE		
AMBER VALLEY	112,800	2,160
BOLSOVER	71,300	1,270
CHESTERFIELD	100,300	1,900
DERBY	225,400	3,990
EREWASH	107,500	1,890
HIGH PEAK	86,100	1,500
NORTH EAST DERBYSHIRE	98,800	1,650
SOUTH DERBYSHIRE	72,900	1,210
THE DERBYSHIRE DALES	68,100	1,420
DERBYSHIRE TOTAL	**943,200**	**16,990**
LEICESTERSHIRE		
BLABY	83,400	1,330
CHARNWOOD	147,600	2,450
HARBOROUGH	68,200	1,170
HINCKLEY & BOSWORTH	97,200	1,640
LEICESTER	284,700	4,940
MELTON	45,500	790
NORTH WEST LEICESTERSHIRE	81,400	1,400
OADBY & WIGSTON	53,100	860
RUTLAND	33,200	550
LEICESTERSHIRE TOTAL	**894,300**	**15,130**
LINCOLNSHIRE		
BOSTON	53,600	1,120
EAST LINDSEY	118,000	2,670
LINCOLN	84,800	1,510
NORTH KESTEVEN	80,100	1,560
SOUTH HOLLAND	67,800	1,420
SOUTH KESTEVEN	110,100	1,930
WEST LINDSEY	76,700	1,400
LINCOLNSHIRE TOTAL	**591,100**	**11,610**

	Total Population	Estimated B & PS Population
NORFOLK		
BRECKLAND	108,300	2,240
BROADLAND	107,200	2,150
GREAT YARMOUTH	88,900	1,880
NORTH NORFOLK	92,000	2,470
NORWICH	127,200	2,510
SOUTH NORFOLK	104,100	2,120
KINGS LYNN & WEST NORFOLK	131,700	2,800
NORFOLK TOTAL	**759,400**	**16,170**
NORTHAMPTON		
CORBY	53,600	720
DAVENTRY	63,000	990
EAST NORTHAMPTONSHIRE	68,600	1,260
KETTERING	77,000	1,450
NORTHAMPTON	184,600	3,010
SOUTH NORTHAMPTONSHIRE	71,100	1,140
WELLINGBOROUGH	68,600	1,160
NORTHAMPTON TOTAL	**586,500**	**9,73,0**
NOTTINGHAMSHIRE		
ASHFIELD	109,700	1,830
BASSETLAW	105,300	1,790
BROXTOWE	108,800	1,870
GEDLING	111,200	1,910
MANSFIELD	101,600	1,700
NEWARK & SHERWOOD	103,700	1,840
NOTTINGHAM	280,900	4,910
RUSHCLIFFE	99,000	1,820
NOTTINGHAMSHIRE TOTAL	**1,020,200**	**17,670**
SUFFOLK		
BABERGH	80,500	1,540
FOREST HEATH	59,600	920
IPSWICH	118,800	2,320
MID SUFFOLK	79,200	1,500
ST EDMUNDSBURY	92,700	1,660
SUFFOLK COASTAL	114,600	2,420
WAVENEY	108,300	2,540
SUFFOLK TOTAL	**653,700**	**12,900**
TOTAL EAST MIDLANDS	**6,117,100**	**111,200**

Table 5 (vi) **The blind and partially sighted population of England by local authority administrative unit. West Midlands Region**

	Total Population	Estimated B & PS Population
HEREFORD AND WORCESTER		
BROMSGROVE	92,200	1,580
HEREFORD	51,000	960
LEOMINSTER	40,000	900
MALVERN HILLS	88,600	2,000
REDDITCH	79,000	980
SOUTH HEREFORDSHIRE	52,100	1,060
WORCESTER	84,500	1,430
WYCHAVON	102,300	1,900
WYRE FOREST	95,700	1,680
HEREFORD AND WORCESTER TOTAL	**685,400**	**12,490**
SHROPSHIRE		
BRIDGNORTH	50,700	900
NORTH SHROPSHIRE	53,600	1,030
OSWESTRY	34,500	680
SHREWSBURY & ATCHAM	92,300	1,730
SOUTH SHROPSHIRE	38,600	870
THE WREKIN	141,900	2,000
SHROPSHIRE TOTAL	**411,600**	**7,210**
STAFFORDSHIRE		
CANNOCK CHASE	90,000	1,220
EAST STAFFORDSHIRE	98,400	1,690
LICHFIELD	93,200	1,410
NEWCASTLE-UNDER-LYME	121,800	2,170
SOUTH STAFFORDSHIRE	106,300	1,530
STAFFORD	119,800	2,110
STAFFORDSHIRE MOORLANDS	96,100	1,660
STOKE-ON-TRENT	253,100	4,290
TAMWORTH	71,000	810
STAFFORDSHIRE TOTAL	**1,049,700**	**16,890**
WARWICKSHIRE		
NORTH WARWICKSHIRE	61,300	940
NUNEATON & BEDWORTH	118,200	1,760
RUGBY	85,500	1,520
STRATFORD-ON-AVON	105,900	2,100
WARWICK	118,300	2,200
WARWICKSHIRE TOTAL	**489,200**	**8,520**

	Total Population	Estimated B & PS Population
WEST MIDLANDS		
BIRMINGHAM	1,006,500	17,260
COVENTRY	305,600	5,270
DUDLEY	309,400	5,180
SANDWELL	294,800	5,300
SOLIHULL	201,200	3,260
WALSALL	263,400	4,190
WOLVERHAMPTON	248,500	4,270
WEST MIDLANDS TOTAL	**2,629,400**	**44,730**
TOTAL WEST MIDLANDS	**5,265,300**	**89,840**

Table 5 (vii) The blind and partially sighted population of England by local authority administrative unit. North East Region

	Total Population	Estimated B & PS Population
CLEVELAND		
HARTLEPOOL	91,500	1,470
LANGBAURGH-ON-TEES	146,400	2,340
MIDDLESBROUGH	146,400	2,140
STOCKTON-ON-TEES	175,400	2,530
CLEVELAND TOTAL	**559,700**	**8,480**
DURHAM		
CHESTER-LE-STREET	53,2001	840
DARLINGTON	99,900	1,890
DERWENTSIDE	87,000	1,640
DURHAM	87,000	1,370
EASINGTON	99,100	1,650
SEDGEFIELD	91,600	1,470
TEESDALE	24,500	510
WEAR VALLEY	63,400	1,210
DURHAM TOTAL	**605,700**	**10,580**
HUMBERSIDE		
BEVERLEY	113,200	2,230
BOOTHFERRY	64,700	1,130
CLEETHORPES	69,800	1,180
GLANFORD	72,200	1,210
GREAT GRIMSBY	91,900	1,610
HOLDERNESS	51,400	920
KINGSTON UPON HULL	266,500	4,500
EAST YORKSHIRE	85,300	1,910
SCUNTHORPE	62,400	1,060
HUMBERSIDE TOTAL	**877,400**	**15,750**
NORTHUMBERLAND		
ALNWICK	30,300	640
BERWICK-UPON-TWEED	26,800	590
BLYTH VALLEY	80,300	1,180
CASTLE MORPETH	50,200	970
TYNEDALE	57,400	1,160
WANSBECK	61,600	1,130
NORTHUMBERLAND TOTAL	**306,600**	**5,670**

	Total Population	Estimated B & PS Population
TYNE & WEAR		
GATESHEAD	203,100	3,630
NEWCASTLE UPON TYNE	278,200	5,210
NORTH TYNESIDE	195,500	3,660
SOUTH TYNESIDE	157,200	2,790
SUNDERLAND	296,400	4,690
TYNE & WEAR TOTAL	**1,130,400**	**19,980**
YORKSHIRE		
BARNSLEY	224,400	3,860
DONCASTER	293,300	4,800
ROTHERHAM	254,900	4,090
SHEFFIELD	529,300	10,430
BRADFORD	475,400	7,960
CALDERDALE	194,000	3,610
KIRKLEES	381,500	6,550
LEEDS	717,400	12,850
WAKEFIELD	316,200	5,070
CRAVEN	50,700	1,170
HAMBLETON	79,500	1,460
HARROGATE	145,400	3,130
RICHMONDSHIRE	46,100	750
RYEDALE	91,400	1,840
SCARBOROUGH	109,200	2,680
SELBY	92,400	1,490
YORK	104,400	2,060
YORKSHIRE TOTAL	**4,105,500**	**73,800**
NORTH EAST TOTAL	**7,585,300**	**134,260**

**Table 5 (viii)   The blind and partially sighted population of England by local authority administrative unit.
Merseyside**

	Total Population	Estimated B & PS Population
DISTRICT COUNCILS		
KNOWSLEY	156,900	2,130
LIVERPOOL	480,700	8,460
ST HELENS	180,900	2,950
SEFTON	295,200	6,040
WIRRAL	336,000	6,680
WEST LANCASHIRE	109,400	1,720
WARRINGTON	185,200	2,910
HALTON	124,900	1,720
ELLESMERE PORT & NESTON	81,500	1,250
TOTAL MERSEYSIDE	**1,950,700**	**33,860**

Table 5 (ix) The blind and partially sighted population of England by local authority administrative unit. North West Region

	Total Population	Estimated B & PS Population
CHESHIRE		
CHESTER	118,000	2,220
CONGLETON	85,300	1,460
CREWE & NANTWICH	105,400	1,850
MACCLESFIELD	151,300	2,900
VALE ROYAL	114,500	1,890
CHESHIRE TOTAL	**574,500**	**10,320**
CUMBRIA		
ALLERDALE	96,700	1,800
BARROW-IN-FURNESS	73,700	1,280
CARLISLE	101,900	1,950
COPELAND	72,000	1,150
EDEN	46,000	920
SOUTH LAKELAND	98,900	2,320
CUMBRIA TOTAL	**489,200**	**9,420**
GREATER MANCHESTER		
BOLTON	262,900	4,510
BURY	179,100	3,140
MANCHESTER	438,500	7,470
OLDHAM	219,600	3,770
ROCHDALE	204,800	3,370
SALFORD	230,900	4,300
STOCKPORT	288,300	5,200
TAMESIDE	219,800	3,780
TRAFFORD	215,800	3,930
WIGAN	310,900	4,850
GREATER MANCHESTER TOTAL	**2,570,600**	**44,320**

	Total Population	Estimated B & PS Population
LANCASHIRE		
BLACKBURN	137,900	2,320
BLACKPOOL	149,800	3,570
BURNLEY	92,200	1,670
CHORLEY	97,100	1,550
FYLDE	72,300	1,880
HYNDBURN	79,000	1,430
LANCASTER	130,100	2,900
PENDLE	85,800	1,630
PRESTON	131,700	2,290
RIBBLE VALLEY	52,100	1,020
ROSSENDALE	66,200	1,150
SOUTH RIBBLE	103,000	1,620
WYRE	103,100	2,460
LANCASHIRE TOTAL	**1,300,300**	**25,490**
TOTAL NORTH WEST	**4,934,600**	**89,550**

Sources: General

- Barnes C: *Disabled People in Britain and Discrimination.* London, Hurst and Co BCODP, 1991.

- Bookbinder D: *Housing Options for Older People.* London, Age Concern, 1991.

- Bruce, McKennel, Walker: *Blind and Partially Sighted Adults in Britain – The RNIB Needs Survey Volume 1.* London, HMSO, 1991.

- Buckle J R, Walker: *Work and Housing of Impaired Persons in Great Britain.* London, OPCS HMSO, 1971.

- Bynoe I, Oliver M, Barnes C: *Equal Rights for Disabled People.* London, Institute of Public Research, 1992.

- Chartered Institute of Housing: *More than Bricks and Mortar.* Coventry, Chartered Institute of Housing, 1993.

- Department of Environment: *Housing Services for Disabled People.* London, 1978.

- Finkelstein V: *Attitudes and Disabled People: Issues for Discussion (Rehabilitation).* 1980.

- Housing Corporation: *Annual Report 1991/92.* London, Housing Corporation, 1991.

- Housing Corporation: *Housing Needs Indicators.* London, Housing Corporation, 1988.

- Housing Corporation: *Performance Audit Visit Manual.* London, Housing Corporation, 1992.

- Housing Corporation: *The Housing Needs Indicator 1990/91.* London, Housing Corporation, 1990.

- Mathews J: *Handicapped People: The Newest Militant Minority?* Braille Forum, 1975.

- MacKintosh S, Means R, Leather P: *Housing in Later Life.* Bristol, Saus.

- Martin J, White A: *OPCS Surveys of Disability in Great Britain.* London, HMSO, 1988.

- Martin J, Meltzer H, Elliot D: *The Prevalence of Disability among Adults.* London, OPCS, 1988.

- Minors M: *Housing for the Disabled in Greater London.* London, GLC research memorandum 462, 1975.

- Morris J: *Pride against Prejudice – Transforming Attitudes to Disability.* London, Women's Press, 1991.

- *Attitudes and Disabled People: Issues for Discussion (Rehabilitation).* 1980.

- Morris J: *Freedom to Lose: Housing Policy and People with Disabilities.* London, Shelter, 1988.

- Morris J: *Our Home: Our Rights.* London, Shelter, 1990.

- Office of Public Management: *Assessment of the Housing Requirements of People with Special Needs over the next Decade.* London, NFHA, 1992.

- Oliver M: *The Politics of Disablement.* London, MacMillan, 1990.

- Oliver M: *Physical Disability: Society's Handicap, Community Care,* 1981.

- Penton & Barlow: *A Handbook of Housing for Disabled People.* London, RADAR, 1981.

- Randolph B: *Housing People with Special Needs, Research Report 13.* London, NFHA, 1990.

- RADAR: *Towards a Housing Policy for Disabled People.* London, RADAR, 1976.

- Rickelman B, Blaylock J: *Behaviours of Sighted Individuals Perceived by Blind Persons as Hindrances to Self Reliance in Blind Persons, Journal of Visual Impairment and Blindness – Volume 77.* 1983.

- Rowe A: *Lifetime Homes: Flexible Housing for Successive Generations.* London, 1990.

- Shore P: *Local Authority Social Rehabilitation Services to Visually Handicapped People.* London, RNIB, 1985.

- Soder M: *Prejudice or Ambivalence?: Attitudes Towards Persons with Disabilities.* Disability, Handicap & Society, 1990.

- Sutherland A T: *Disabled we Stand.* London, Souvenir Press, 1981.

- Walbrook Housing Association: *Cracking Housing Problems Faced by Disabled People.* Derby, Walbrook Housing Association, 1992.

- Ward A L: *The Response to Individuals Beginning Work with Blind Persons, The New Outlook for the Blind – Volume 67.* 1993.

- Warriner C: *The Handicaps of Sighted Persons, Journal of Visual Impairment and Blindness – Volume 73.* 1979.

Sources: Design

- Access Committee for England: *Building Homes for Successive Generations.* London, Access Committee for England, 1992.

- British Standards Institute: *BS5619 Design of Housing for the Convenience of Disabled People.* British Standards Institute, 1978.

- Bristow A, Rutherford A: *A Survey of Housing Designed for People who have a Physical Disability.* London, Department of Environment, 1979.

- Colquhoun I, Shepherd J: *Housing for Disabled People.* Institute of Housing, RIBA, 1988.

- Department of Environment: *House Adaptations for People with Physical Disabilities.* London, HMSO.

- European Committee for Access to the Built Environment: *European Manual for an Accessible Built Environment.* CCPT, 1990.

- London Borough of Islington: *Housing for People with Disabilities, a Design Guide.* London, London Borough of Islington Architectural Department, 1989.

- Goldsmith S: *Designing for the Disabled.* London, RIBA, 1976.

- Thorpe S: *Designing for People with Sensory Impairments.* London, Access Committee for England, 1990.

- Partially Sighted Society: *Providing for People with Impaired Vision: Access Guide.* Partially Sighted Society, 1985.

This report is part of a new **research** series from the Housing Management and Research Division of the Housing Corporation, launched in 1995.

Currently available titles are:

1. Housing association involvement in mortgage rescue
   an evaluation of the initiatives

   (ISBN 0 901454 59 1)

   HACAS Published February 1995 Price £10

2. Do-it-yourself shared ownership: an evaluation

   (ISBN 0 901454 60 5)

   Glen Bramley, Kathleen Dunmore, Claire Durrant and Gavin Smart

   Published February 1995 Price £10

3. HAMA: managing the private rented sector
   a comparison of housing associations and private managing agents

   (ISBN 0 901454 61 3)

   London Research Centre Published February 1995 Price £10

4. Social housing over shops evaluated

   (ISBN 0 901454 62 1)

   Oliver Chamberlain, Barry Goodchild, Sheffield Hallam University

   Published February 1995 Price £10

5. The Housing Corporation's implementation of the Housing Market Package

   (ISBN 0 901454 63 X)

   Touche Ross Management Consultants
   Published February 1995 Price £10

6. The housing needs of people with a visual impairment

   (ISBN 0 901454 57 5)

   Royal National Institute for the Blind
   Published February 1995 Price £10

There are additional research publications available from the Housing Corporation, published before 1995. Reports and full publications lists can be ordered from the Publications Department, The Housing Corporation, 149 Tottenham Court Road, London W1P 0BN. Tel: 0171 393 2000 Fax: 0171 393 2111. Please send a written order and cheque in advance made payable to "The Housing Corporation".